Brothers & Sisters

Brothers & Sisters

Getting Back Together With Your Adult Siblings

Barbara L. Johnson

Prometheus Books • Buffalo, New York

To Bill and Doreene—my siblings

Published 1991 by Prometheus Books

95 94 93 92 91   5 4 3 2 1

Library of Congress Cataloging-in-Publication Data

Johnson, Barbara L.
    Brothers & sisters: getting back together with your
adult siblings / by Barbara L. Johnson.
        p.   cm.
    ISBN 0-87975-682-9
    1. Brothers and sisters. 2. Adulthood—Psychological
aspects. I. Title. II. Title: Brothers and sisters.
BF723.S43J64   1991
158'.24—dc20   91-27898
                                                              CIP

Printed in the United States of America on acid-free paper.

Acknowledgments

My sincere appreciation to the many people I stopped to interview in Golden Gate Park, San Francisco. They told me about their sibling experiences, both happy and sad. I do not know their names, but without their help this book would not have been possible.

The names of the people in this book, and some of the details of their stories, have been changed in order to protect their privacy.

Contents

1

Siblings Lost and Found

As children were you and your siblings close? Was a brother or sister the person who knew you best in the world? Did you always plan to keep in touch with that sibling, but somehow years and distances pulled you apart? Today, maybe your friends and acquaintances occupy your days, but do these relationships quite fill the special place once held by a brother or a sister? Your sibling was the person who . . .

- knew you when your life was forming,
- shared the parents that shaped your being,
- was privy to the secrets of your early loves,
- tried to help you through your first sorrows,
- encouraged even your most outrageous ambitions,
- told you when you were out of line and helped you to get back on track.

You and your sibling promised you would always be there for one another, and then time and circumstances separated you.

Where is that special brother or sister now? How long has it been since you have written or spoken to your sibling? Are you thinking that too much time has gone by and you have drifted too far apart to experience the closeness you once enjoyed? Or have you made an attempt to reach out that has ended in failure?

Reconciliation may not be easy, and at first all the effort may be on your side, but with work, patience, and persistence the renewal of kin caring can become a reality. This book is for the millions of adult brothers and sisters who would like to make that journey back to sibling closeness.

Although adult sibling separation is a common problem, little has been written for the lay person about how to bridge the gap between childhood intimacy and adult alienation. Most sibling guides, written by psychologists and psychiatrists, approach the subject of adult sibling relations from a clinical and abstract viewpoint. Such books often dwell heavily on problems and abnormal behavior. This handbook, very different in approach and the first of its kind, takes an uncomplicated and down-to-earth look at the subject of kin caring. Over a decade of research and 200 interviews have gone into this project. Many case histories taken from these interviews are used throughout the text to illustrate suggested ideas and advice. From the hearts and minds of adult brothers and sisters, who gave me their time and told me their joys and sorrows, come the suggestions that can help you find your way back to sibling closeness.

Sadly, the comment I heard most often was one of regret. It came from siblings who had waited too long to try to renew their relationship with a beloved brother or sister and were left to say their goodbyes at a graveside. As long as your siblings live it is not too late to try to get back together.

That is what this book is all about.

Some of the Ways These Pages Will Work for You

Since no two sibling relationships are the same, some suggestions offered in this guide will be more useful for your unique situation than others. Ideas that may work for you and one sibling may not work for you and another sibling. Choose the suggestions you think will help you with each separate renewal plan.

Here are just a few of the suggestions and strategies you will find in the chapters that follow.

Guides for Measuring Relationship Quality

There is a special section to help you measure the quality of your present relationships with your siblings.

Maybe you think your siblings like you, but this is just a guess on your part because you don't know them all that well anymore. Or maybe you have the feeling that you and your siblings aren't close at all. Or maybe you have no idea how your siblings feel about you. Questions included in special self-tests will help you determine:

- whether your relationship status with any one of your siblings is affected by acts and attitudes left over from the past,
- whether your current sibling contacts are damaging or helping your relationship with your siblings,
- how you honestly feel about your siblings,
- how your siblings feel about you.

Problem-Solving Suggestions

No relationship, however caring and honest, is ever totally free of problems—sibling relationships are no exception. Maybe there are problems between you and your sibling left over from childhood. Or maybe there's a new set of problems between you that came up recently. If you don't try to do something to solve these problems, they won't get any better.

The section on problem solving will help to guide you toward wise solutions to both minor and major problems including:

- problems created by your sibling;
- problems brought on by family, friends, and others;
- you as the problem;
- problems that relate to the times—such as distances, divorce, job pressures, and greed.

What Makes a Poor Sibling Relationship?

There is a special section on what makes a poor sibling relationship.

Maybe you will recognize yourself in this section. Some siblings do so many things to alienate one another it is a wonder they speak at all. Siblings . . .

- correct one another,
- try to get the best of one another,
- put each other down for real and imagined shortcomings,
- bring up old grievances,
- make unfavorable comparisons.

The list of things siblings do to hurt each other could go on for pages, and each one of these mistakes could become a pitfall for relationship success. Finding out about what not to do can be good insurance for starting out right.

What Makes a Good Sibling Relationship?

There is a special section on what makes a good sibling relationship.

Listed here are stories from sibilngs who help one another, listen to one another, and are close when comfort is needed. Copying what is right about sibling relationships may help you renew your closeness to your brothers and sisters. By trying out the success formulas offered in this section, you may find your own path to sibling closeness.

Planning and Timing Suggestions

There is a section on getting organized and planning a sibling relationship campaign.

Making one phone call, writing one letter, or getting something right once, does not a reconciliation make. Success calls for renewal of these efforts built up deed upon deed, day upon day. It is easy to overlook or put off good intentions, or even to lose track of them in the maze of everyday activities. Weeks and months can go by between calls, visits, or letters before you realize you have lapsed unless you keep a calendar of closeness. Why not schedule something as important as your sibling contacts? This section on planning and timing offers suggestions for setting up a calendar of sibling relationship renewal plans. Dependability is a very important key to sibling closeness. Being a person worthy of trust sometimes takes some scheduling.

Communication Conduct

The importance of two-way communication, with strong emphasis on listening instead of talking, is illustrated in this section by using examples of "cat and dog" listeners. An added self-test at the end of the chapter will help you rate your sibling-communication skills.

A Sibling Code of Ethics

Ethics are those invisible guidelines that keep you from losing your sense of direction in today's precariously uncertain world. The section on sibling ethics will help you to make the sometimes tough but right decisions needed for you and your siblings to lead a better life together.

Not a hair-shirt lecture, this section is designed to help you measure your own personal values and design your own unique code of conduct. A part on the hidden rewards of good ethics points out the many ways that using these guidelines will change your life for the better.

The ABC's of Relationship Suggestions

There is a section, set up as a glossary, containing all of the practical suggestions that appear throughout the book. Better than an index, this list of terms, defined in relationship to sibling caring, carries the essence of the book's lessons. You can return to these pages again and again to renew and refresh your memory of the advice offered in this guide.

Not the End, Just the Beginning

Only a few of the sections and a fraction of the contents of the book have been reviewed in this chapter. The aim has been to offer you a road map of your journey toward sibling-relationship renewal, to give you an idea of what help to expect and to warn you about the kinds of hurdles you should anticipate. Armed with this knowledge you can do a much better job of learning and renewing.

Chapter 1 in a Nutshell

As long as your siblings live, it is never too late to try to get back together.

Some of the tools to renewed sibling relationships offered in this book include:

- guides for measuring relationship quality,
- problem solving suggestions,
- a list of common denominators of poor sibling relationships,
- a list of common denominators of good sibling relationships,
- planning and timing suggestions,
- communication conduct,
- a sibling code of ethics,
- a glossary of sibling relationship suggestions.

2

Willie Pig, I Need You

You can go back to sibling closeness. You can renew the ties you had with your siblings before time and circumstances separated you. The path to sibling reconciliation may be difficult to find and arduous to follow, but that path is there. And like little white stones dropped at your feet, the clues to closeness are strewn along the way.

This story of Willie Pig illustrates how one brother, listening with his heart, picked up on a single clue that turned out to be a cry for help.

A call for help may come in many ways

I watched from the window until I saw the mail jeep turn the corner, and then I went down to see what had been left in my mailbox. I was hoping my favorite sports magazine would be delivered and I'd have something to do with the empty afternoon that stretched in front of me. There had been a time when Saturday was my busy day.

As usual the box was stuffed with junk mail. I looked over a pizza advertisement, a sheet of grocery specials, a mass mailing for health insurance, and two letters asking for donations. There was no magazine. I went out to the kitchen to stuff the whole sheaf of unwanted paper into the garbage sack. As I leaned over, an envelope slipped out from between the pizza ad and the grocery special sheet and fell at my feet.

The way the envelope was addressed made it look like a personal letter. The address was written in a hand that looked vaguely familiar. The postmark said San Francisco. I turned the envelope over and studied the return address written on the back. The return address said San Francisco, too. Instead of opening the envelope to find out what was inside, I stood in the kitchen speculating about whom I knew way out in California. Finally I took the letter and went back to my window chair. I ripped open the flap and pulled out a folded sheet of pale blue paper, but even then I didn't open the paper to read the message inside. I received so little personal mail these days I guess I was savoring the moment. Of course, I had a hunch the thing could turn out to be a gimmick, some smart advertising trick. When I finally did open the paper, the letter inside came as a complete surprise. I hadn't heard from my sister in years.

Dear Willie Pig,

How are you? I hope you are at the same address and this letter finds you. It has been a very long time since we have been in touch. As you can see by my address, I am now living in San Francisco. That's where Ed finally dumped me. I should have known. But that's another story.

Have you ever thought about taking a trip out this way? I would like to see you. Of course, maybe you've remarried. I suppose you are as busy as ever.

The other day I was thinking about our old dog Oliver and how we took turns letting him sleep in our bed. Remember how he used to crawl under the covers and snuggle way down to the bottom of the bed? Best foot warmer I ever had.

Well, just thought I'd say hello. Drop me a line if you have time. I'll be here.

Love, Helen

I read the letter a second time, and then again. Then I got to my feet, moving faster than I had in weeks. In less than an hour I had a plane reservation, my bag was packed, and I'd gotten my boss on the line and asked for a few days off. There was nothing complicated about closing up my apartment. I didn't even own a plant to water. I stopped by my landlady's unit and asked if she would take in my mail. Then I was off.

The address Helen had given me in San Francisco was in a distinctly down-and-out part of town, no mistake. Time zones do funny things to my head, but I knew I couldn't be that fuzzy. I'd taken a cab right from the airport, not knowing it was so far to the city. When I paid the driver he looked at the wad of cash I stuffed back into my wallet. I'd brought all the emergency funds I kept hidden at home. "Better keep that dough in a safe place," he said. It was then I took a second look around at where I was.

Most of the buildings on the block were boarded up or protected with iron window and door grates. The sidewalk was scattered with an accumulation of wind-blown garbage. Several people lolled against buildings. One bundle of rags, which had a faintly human form, was stretched out in the only open doorway on the block. The odor of stale urine and cheap wine hung in the air. I checked the numbers on Helen's letter again. They matched those on the dilapidated building in front of me. Helen couldn't be living here. She just couldn't. Helen was the one who had always said surroundings were more important than food.

I looked more closely at the front of the building and it was then that I noted a small tag stuck beside the mailboxes. The tag contained a list of names and apartment numbers. I scanned the list and my heart sank as I saw Helen's name was there. For a moment I wished I hadn't come, then

I remembered "Dear Willie Pig" and I knew she must need me. I reached out and pushed the buzzer, never guessing it would actually work. In less than a minute there was an answering buzz. I pulled at the door and it opened.

Inside, the dim hallway smelled of dust and long-ago cabbage dinners. I started up the stairs. "That you, Fanny?" The question came from directly over my head. I recognized Helen's voice. I looked up in search of my young, auburn-haired sister. A pale and drained-looking woman, with a thin, nearly toothless smile, stared down at me. I must have been wrong about the voice. This couldn't be Helen. "My name is Bill Taylor. I'm looking for Helen Ashburn."

The woman said nothing. She stared at me and then her face began to crumple in despair. "Willie Pig," I heard her sigh. I took the stairs two at a time.

That all happened seven weeks ago. Helen is back with me now. We've got a bigger place, and we even have plants in a window box that Helen likes to fuss over. I have something to do on Saturdays besides wait for a magazine in the mail. In fact, I'm happier than I've been in years.

Of course, it took some convincing to get Helen to come with me. I had a hard time making her see that I needed her as much as she needed me. At first she was convinced that all the need was on her side. Helen always was darned stubborn and full of pride.

"I didn't call for help. I didn't say I needed you," she kept arguing. "But I'm glad you came. How did you know how bad things were?" she finally asked. "How did you know I was in need?"

"It was simple," I told her. "I just remembered the time when you were a little kid and you climbed up in that old apple tree in the backyard. You couldn't get down, but you didn't yell for help.

You called me by the favorite name you had for me—Willie Pig. And then there was the time we went all the way to the ocean beach for a swim. You didn't know anything about waves and undertow and you got swept off your feet. I was sleeping in the sand, but again when I heard you call 'Willie Pig,' I knew you were in trouble."

And that's how we found we needed each other.

Finding a New Closeness with Your Sibling

Maybe your sibling has left a clue for you. Maybe you should let your sibling know you are in need. Siblings can go a lifetime wanting and needing each other and yet stand too proud to admit their needs. Some siblings give out hints that they are in need, but these hints go unnoticed.

- How good are you at reading your sibling's true feelings?
- How good are you at telling your sibling your needs?

Here are just a few examples of some of the wandering and frantic ways siblings have told one another of their needs.

Pregnant at sixty?

I sent my brother a telegram saying, "Come at once. I'm pregnant." He came, which was remarkable considering I'm sixty years old and the message couldn't have possibly been true. But long ago when we parted—that was when we were right out of high school—he had said to me, "If you ever need me, you get pregnant or anything, don't be too proud to call for help." I was a long time calling, but when I needed him he was there.

The grocery tab message

My brother sent me a message. It was written on the back of a grocery tab. All it said was, "I don't need you." When I read the message I looked at the other side of the tab and what I saw left no doubt in my mind—my brother was in trouble. The tab itemized two bottles of jug wine and three six-packs of beer. My brother's an alcoholic who hasn't had a drink for years. The grocery tab was a cry for help—his way of saying he needed me.

The Queen and Essex

My brother sent me a dime-store ring. With it was a note that said, "Dear Queen, I love you. Signed, Essex." As children my brother and I had loved the story of Queen Elizabeth I who had given the Earl of Essex a ring to send to her if he was in trouble and needed her help. Although the real Essex never sent the ring and was beheaded for treason, I was able to help my brother in a time of need.

Three birch trees

I sent my sister a note saying, "Birch trees are dying." I hoped with all my heart that she knew what I meant. Even as a child I had always said when I found a place where I was happy, I would plant three birch trees and settle down for life. When I moved to the farm in Oregon I planted my three birch. My sister wasn't sure a farm was a place where I could be happy. I was a Chicago girl, and she knew I liked living in the city. She was right about my not fitting in as a country girl, but somehow I was too proud to come right out and admit that she had been right. She recognized my "birch tree" message as a cry for help and came to my rescue with a rental moving van.

Are You Listening for Clues?

Maybe you have a sibling who needs you. Or maybe your life, however busy, seems a little empty. Wouldn't it be wonderful to get back to the close ties you and your siblings had as children? Send your sibling a message. Or maybe you've heard from your sibling recently. Did you try reading between the lines? Maybe your sibling may be trying to tell you something without having to come right out and shout it.

Of course, finding your way back to family closeness may not be easy. And there is always the possibility that your sibling may not be as keen on closeness as you are. If long periods of time and great differences have come between you and your brothers and sisters, you will certainly have to work at renewed happiness. But aren't all gains usually in direct proportion to the amount of effort put into seeking them?

If you are willing to take the time and make the effort that may be needed to reach back across a void of years, your reward will be a relationship even greater than your best memories. Start looking for those white pebbles. Maybe your sibling has been trying to reach you.

Chapter 2 in a Nutshell

- Your sibling's call for help may come in many ways.
- Finding your way back to sibling closeness sometimes calls for listening to your heart.

3

Siblings Need Each Other

You can write the script for your days, calling for a full and rounded life, but willingly or unwillingly you have to go along with the way the world presents the play. Life's true performance is almost never like the rehearsal.

One day your life can be busy with friends, a happy marriage, an interesting job. Your hours are full and satisfying. Then suddenly, like water seeping through dry sand, the good things in your life can drain away. Friends move, marriages come apart, jobs end, bad health confines you, and your parents die, but if you have a living sibling, your life need never be empty. Your sibling can be someone to turn to when everything goes wrong and everyone else turns away. Hold that thought while you read about some of the things that can happen to a busy life that supposedly would never change.

Friendship Is Not a Lifetime Guarantee

Friendships are not bound by ironclad contracts that cannot be broken. You choose your friends and they choose you, but the door of friendship swings both ways, and through that door friends can enter and they can leave again. Sometimes friends get tired of you. Sometimes friends die. Sometimes, as in the following story, friends move away.

They moved away and forgot us

A weekend spent without Charley and Jen was unthinkable. The four of us were always together. If there was a ball game we went together and then shared a potluck dinner together afterward. Parties, fishing trips, and vacations were planned by and for the four of us. Even the night of the big snowstorm Jen and Charley walked to our place. We dragged out the sleeping bags and they stayed the weekend. We were all sure that nothing would ever come between us. We seldom saw our other friends, and we all but forgot we ever had brothers and sisters.

When Charley got his promotion we celebrated, but the festivities ended suddenly when his company asked him to take a new territory halfway across the country. Next thing we knew everything Charley and Jen owned was in a rental truck, and we were left standing at the curb waving goodby. In our first days of desperate loneliness, Mary and I even talked about moving after them, but that would have meant leaving our jobs and taking our chances on finding something new.

We still write letters but our notes are getting shorter and further and further apart. The first year after Jen and Charley moved we still planned a vacation together, but for some reason the trip never panned out. There's a hole in our lives where they used to be. I guess we could make new friends, but maybe they'd just move on, too.

Friendships, however close, are always tentative. Friends can . . .

- move away,

- grow apart in interests,
- disagree,
- die.

One day friends can fill your life and the next they can be gone.

Marriages Don't Always Last

The vows of marriage can be commitments that fail. One day there is a promise and then the promise is broken, as this story illustrates.

My marriage failed

When Paul and I were married I thought my life was complete. His family became my family and his friends were mine, too. I didn't need anyone or anything else.

When girlfriends from my single days telephoned about a get-together, I was always too busy with Paul's friends to make time to see them.

When my brother Ted came to visit us, he and Paul didn't seem to hit it off so I never invited my brother again.

We moved to Paul's hometown and saw a lot of Paul's parents but none of mine.

Then, one day, all that was over. It's strange how I can remember the little details about the moment my marriage came to an end. I'd just washed my hair and stepped dripping wet from the shower when Paul came into the bathroom. I grinned at him but he didn't smile back. Instead, in a rush of words, while I stood there dripping, he told me he wanted out of our marriage. He said he had been trying for a long time to tell me he'd found someone else. I couldn't find my voice to answer him. I just got back in the shower and let the water run while I cried and cried. When I finally came out of the bathroom Paul was gone.

I was too proud to go back to my old friends, or even my family. I just couldn't face any of them. And, of course, Paul's friends went with Paul. They were part of the divorce settlement I guess. At any rate, I'm more alone now than I ever thought I could be.

An increasing number of marriages are not lasting until "death us do part."

A spouse can . . .

- find someone else,
- put a career ahead of marriage,
- decide a single life is best,
- change interests.

One day your marriage can make you willing to give up everything else in life, and then the marriage dies and you have nothing.

Job Security Is a Modern Myth

Thirty years with the same company and a gold watch upon retirement is a "once upon a time" story in today's working environment. Mergers, buy-outs, bankruptcy, and politics can put an end to companies and budding careers. The strong are perishing with the weak in company moves. Job security is a thing of the past. Workers who make their job their entire existence sometimes come up with an empty life, as this story illustrates.

I put everything I had into my job

The office came alive every day at eight-thirty but I was always at my desk before seven. My coffee breaks consisted of a quick gulp from a paper mug of barely warm liquid that was often forgotten at the back of my desk.

Work came ahead of everything including my family, my marriage, my friends, even my health. Then one morning the CEO came into the department and announced that due to curtailment of company funds our whole division was being cut. We were to be given severance pay and job counseling, but our desks were to be cleaned off by the end of the week.

At first I couldn't believe the cut meant me too. I figured one or two of us would be told we were being transferred to other divisions. I waited to be called upstairs to hear where I was going.

I was going out the door, that was where I was going. There was no call upstairs. Ten years of work, of sublimating every other interest in my life to devote my time to my job, was all down the drain. I wasn't any better off than the guy who goofed off and played golf on company time every Friday afternoon.

No job, however hard you work, is eternal. Even when your work is satisfactory, jobs can end when . . .

- companies are sold,
- a new manager is hired,
- management structure is reorganized,
- a more qualified employee comes along.

One day a job can fill your life and the next you can be in the unemployment line.

Poor Health Can Be a Prison

Not just the elderly find themselves confined by poor health. The young can suffer from the loneliness of the forced isolation that illness can bring. Accidents, disease, or hereditary weaknesses can take their toll at any age, as this story illustrates.

Health problems closed in on me

I have plenty of time to think now. I'm not going far from this chair. Do you know what I think about? Not about my accident. No use dwelling on that. No, I think about my sister, Pat, and all the times she phoned me and I was too busy to listen.

I've been a rotten sister since the day Pat was born. I was ten when I was presented with a baby sister. I hated her from day one. She reminded me of a squirming pink worm as she lay in my mother's arms. I went on hating Pat all the years we were growing up. When I left home I never gave her another thought except for those times she phoned me. Then, when I determined it was Pat on the other end of the line, all I could think about was inventing some excuse to cut her off as soon as possible.

It's too late to turn to Pat now. What have I to offer her? I won't let myself do that. I should have been a better sister when I still had two legs to play tennis with her, to hike with her, to go shopping with her . . .

For many people health problems become a prison. Problems like . . .

- decreasing eyesight can make it impossible to drive;
- deafness can end give-and-take conversations;
- lameness can limit shopping trips, golf games, or even the chance to chase after a puppy.

Poor health can bring the added pain of empty hours when friends who no longer see you forget to look you up.

Parents Die

The joy of having parents and a large family circle of aunts and uncles turns into grief when they die. But siblings can usually count on one another to be around to share some of the later days of each other's lives. Siblings can be there for one another when the family circle grows smaller. And siblings, having shared their childhood, can better understand the loss of older members of the family and comfort each other when experiencing the grief of their parent's death.

I took care of Mother

When my brother and sister got married and moved away, I stayed on in the family home with our widowed mother. She and I shared everything in life together. We went shopping, liked the same movies, and even read the same books. When my siblings came to visit, I resented their intrusion into our lives. I made it clear that I'd just as soon they didn't come. Then one day mother had a fall, and a week later she was gone. My brother couldn't make it to the funeral, and my sister stayed only one day with me and flew back to her family. My mother's house is now as empty as my life.

Good parents are your joy while they are with you. You are meant to honor them, but life's pattern makes it very possible that they will die before you do. Don't let love for your parents cause you to exclude your siblings.

Sibling Ties Need Never Come Undone

Lives that are busy one day may be nothing of the sort the next. Things like friendships and jobs can come unraveled, but blood ties—your sibling ties, however far they are stretched—need never come undone.

Your life need not take a turn toward emptiness before you think about getting back together with your siblings. As adults you can rediscover your sibling ties even if your life is full. Siblings can be a bonus to a full life or the remaining comfort when other things in your life have emptied out.

Chapter 3 in a Nutshell

Busy lives can empty out leaving siblings in need of each other.

- Friendships can be uncertain and tentative.
- Marriages don't always last.
- Having a job today is no guarantee that you will be employed tomorrow.
- Poor health can create invisible walls that cut you off from friends and acquaintances.
- Beloved parents can die.

Siblings can be with you when all other things have drifted away. Blood ties, however far they are stretched, need never come undone.

4

Why Siblings Drift Apart

The most common reason for neglecting a sibling relationship is the assumption that brothers and sisters will always be there, and that, unlike friendships, blood ties need no nurturing. Nothing could be further from the truth. Siblings can feel neglected, have hurt feelings, or grow tired of playing second fiddle just like any other person.

Indifference to the need to make an effort to maintain family closeness is the number one reason siblings drift apart.

Excuses for not maintaining sibling ties string out like a laundry list, beginning and ending with apathy. Siblings drift apart because . . .

- they are indifferent to the destruction created by the passage of time;
- they are too lethargic to make even a halfway effort toward reconciliation;
- they blame outside influences, such as a demanding job, for their neglect;
- they let other people, such as a jealous spouse, come between them;
- they let a contrast in lifestyles divide them;
- they use the difference in their personalities as a wedge;
- they let distance stand between them.

This list could go on and on. Any set of siblings could add their own excuses. The following stories of sibling neglect are typical.

Distance as a Sibling Divider

Distance is used by many as a convenient excuse for not keeping in touch. Miles are blamed for sibling indifference. Oceans and continents divide many families who are scattered throughout the world these days, but despite great distances some siblings do manage to keep their love for one another alive and their information about each other current. Siblings who really want to show their love can overcome any distance that may divide them. Those who are selfish and uncaring can make a mile, or even one block, seem too far to go to see their siblings.

The following story illustrates how distance, even a short one, was used as an excuse for sibling indifference.

Across town was too far

I knew my sister was home alone, that she would welcome a visit from me to break up the loneliness of her day, but I never took the time to drive across town to say hello. I was always going to. I kept telling myself I'd pop in on her the next time I had a moment to spare. Once I even planned a special outing to a shopping mall and lunch together. I never got around to carrying out that plan. I always had some lame excuse like "the weather was too dangerous for driving," or "the roads were pretty crowded that week." Looking back on it now, I realize that it wasn't distance that separated us—my selfishness was the real obstacle.

Time as a Sibling Divider

The passage of time is a great "deteriorator" of sibling closeness, and the more time siblings allow to come between them, the more difficult the task of recovering closeness.

A sibling you haven't seen or talked to in a year can go through many life changes without you ever knowing it. A sibling you haven't seen in ten years can be a totally different person. Time apart from your sibling can drive a wedge of strangeness that eats away at the common ground between you. After a long period of time you may find you have nothing to say to one another.

The following story points out how time can erode caring.

How hours can swallow up the years

Until last week I didn't even know my sister had two children. Not that she wouldn't have written to tell me. I just didn't give her a chance to write. I moved around and never sent back an address. I guess I just didn't want to bother answering letters. I thought about my sister sometimes when I was lonely, like on Christmas when I was far from home. But how could she know I still loved her and that she was in my thoughts? I didn't even send as much as a postcard in seven years. When I finally did drop in on her from out of nowhere, she said she had nothing to say to me anymore.

Life's Clutter Can Get in the Way

Some people are sure they need twenty-five hours in their day to accomplish all the things they think they need to do that no one else can do for them. For people like this there is never any time for siblings. Additional hours in their day would simply allow them to add more clutter to their lives. "Too busy" is an elaborate excuse they use to deceive themselves. Errands, committee meetings, and paperwork are wall-building materials to hide behind.

The following story illustrates how one sibling blinded himself with busyness and lived to regret neglecting his brother.

Learn to take time out

I told myself my family came first. I was sure I loved my brother, but I gave him nothing more than the bare corners of my time. I saw more of my office than I did of my home. I spent more time on a Chamber of Commerce committee than I did with my brother. I never even got around to helping him when his wife got sick. I let the neighbors help instead. Then, one day, one of those neighbors had to call to tell me that my brother had sat down to rest, and his heart was too tired to ever let him get up again. Now I have to live with my regrets.

Lame Excuses Are the Dry Rot of Closeness

Some sibling relationships fall into decay because siblings use lame excuses to cover up the fact that they are too lazy and care too little to take the time to keep in touch. Walking the dog, getting a haircut, listening to TV news, mowing the lawn, and even going to church can all be excuses not to do anything for your sibling.

The following story depicts a typical lightweight excuse.

The birthday card that was never mailed

Last year I saw a birthday card with a picture of the Three Stooges on it. It really brought back some happy memories of all the laughs my brother and I had shared together while watching movies of those guys. I bought the card because my brother's birthday was the following week. That's where the gesture ended. I didn't get around to signing the card and I didn't address the envelope. I told myself I needed to buy a stamp and then I would do it. The real truth is, I'm lazy and uncaring.

Second Guessing Isn't Fair

Made-up and imagined reasons for losing contact with your brothers and sisters aren't reasons at all. Second guessing what your siblings think of you instead of using honest channels of communication isn't fair to anyone—not to you or your sibling. Guesses will never replace the truth, just as guessing will never replace asking.

The story that follows shows how an incorrect supposition can compound itself into a lifetime of separation.

The bad guess

My brother is seven years older than I am. He was always an honor student in high school. I barely squeaked by. He was tall and well built and played varsity football. I was puny and uncoordinated and couldn't have made the checkers team. He married the prettiest girl in town. I had a hard time getting a date. I wanted to be just like my brother, but I always fell so far short, I was intimidated by his shadow.

When my brother left home he never looked back. I was sure he wasn't interested in what happened to me. When I finally graduated from college, when I got a newspaper job, when I was given my first big book contract, I wanted to write and tell him how I was doing and ask him to come celebrate, but I was sure he wouldn't care about my life. One time my sister told me she was sure he was very proud to have an author in the family. Maybe I should have let him answer for himself. We might have had a lot of good times together.

A Spouse Can Drive a Wedge

Siblings can be driven apart by a spouse who tries to come between them. A spouse can be jealous of your sibling and resent the attention you give to him or her. A spouse can form a personality conflict with your sibling and think up new reasons at every renewed contact to drive a new wedge between the two of you. Sometimes a spouse who has trouble relating to people in general may not know how to treat your siblings.

The story that follows sadly relates how repeated attempts by a spouse to drive two siblings apart finally succeeded.

The wife who didn't like her spouse's sibling

Walt may have a few of what some people might call bad habits, like always patting people on the back and talking kinda loud, but I never let that bother me. Walt has so many good qualities they far outweigh the few bothersome things he does. But not everyone feels that way about Walt. My wife says she can't stand him. She's downright rude when she talks to him, too.

After the last time Walt visited our house, my wife said if I ever invited him back she was going out the door the day he came in. I don't know how to tell Walt he can't come back, but I guess if I want to keep my wife I'll have to.

Personality Quirks That Rankle

Certainly not all siblings are perfect. Some brothers and sisters can try their family's patience to the bone. Being human, siblings too are heirs to all kinds of personality quirks. Some belittle, some brag, some tell lies, some chew gum too loud, some are always trying to borrow money. Character quirks and weaknesses on the part of one sibling can annoy even the most patient of siblings and eventually drive them away.

The following story of a chronic complainer illustrates one reason why a fed up sibling may cut the ties.

The chronic complainer

When I invite my sister to dinner she complains that I live better than she does. When I come to visit her she complains that I have better clothes than she can afford. She has aches and pains from her head to her toes and she loves moaning about them. Her neighbors are the most unfair in the city. Her landlady the most unkind. Just once I'd like to hear my sister say something positive. I don't come around as often as I used to. I can't stand her complaining.

Maybe You Are Part of the Problem

Siblings drift apart because there are problems between them, real or imagined, that one or more of the siblings won't make the effort to solve. Don't always blame your sibling. Think about how things look from the other side of the fence. You are part of the problem when:

- you let others come between you and your sibling;
- you excuse yourself from taking steps in your sibling's direction;
- you second guess how your sibling feels and use this as an excuse to do nothing;
- you let bad habits, theirs or yours, stop you from seeing each other.

The tide that allows siblings to drift apart can be turned in the other direction when brothers and sisters learn that excuses are no match for a will to come together again.

- You can keep in touch even over long distances.
- The more often you contact your sibling, the more you will have to say to one another.
- Even the busiest people can spare time for siblings if they have the desire.
- There is no substitute for honest communication between you and your sibling.
- Find ways to see your sibling without the interference or objections of others.
- Remember that you may have some personality quirks that annoy your sibling.

Chapter 4 in a Nutshell

Siblings drift apart because they allow excuses, invented to cover laziness and indifference, to separate them.

Some of the excuses siblings use are:

- distance,
- the passage of time,
- busyness,
- procrastination,
- second guessing,
- a hostile spouse,
- personality quirks.

Two siblings can cause excuses to obstruct their relationship when actually they have a real desire to come together.

5

Common Denominators: Poor Sibling Relationships

All sibling relationships are made up of good and poor experiences. No one relationship is all bad. And, being human, brothers and sisters do not have perfect relationships either. But there are common denominators for those sibling relationships that are good and harmonious, just as there are for those that are poor and indifferent. Most brother and sister relationships fall into the area somewhere between good and poor. Few kinships are all sugar and spice, and few are totally hurtful and bad. In this chapter the factors that contribute to poor sibling relationships are discussed.

A Basic Truth About Poor Relationships

The word "lacking" might best be used to describe what is basically wrong with sibling relationships that fall into the poor or bad category. These relationships "lack" something. People who tend to be self-centered and uncaring in their contacts with their brothers and sisters lack the basic component for good bonding. In such kinships there is no kin caring.

The stories that follow are examples of relationships that have been damaged by unwise siblings who gave too little of themselves and expected too much in return.

Unreliable Siblings

Some siblings promise much and deliver little. Siblings who sprinkle promises throughout their conversation and forget what they have pledged as soon as the sentence dies build relationships as empty as their assurances. When such unreliable siblings occasionally keep their word and show up where they are supposed to be, they often find no one is waiting for them. Wise brothers and sisters who have been stood up times unnumbered learn not to honor thoughtless promises and hollow appointments.

This is the story of just such an unreliable sibling.

I can never depend on him to keep his promises

My brother would keep God waiting. He accepts an invitation to come to my house for dinner and shows up two hours late. I've finally learned to put the food away when he is late and tell him that dinner is over. Even that doesn't seem to give him the message. When he invites me for lunch I eat alone and pay the tab because he forgets to show up. He's the chief customer for those "Sorry I'm Late," type birthday cards. Once he even failed to show up for a vacation we had planned together. Worst of all I got stuck paying for his airline ticket. Now I never take his word for anything.

Impersonal Siblings

Siblings are special to us and they deserve more than group attention. People who are never willing to see a brother or sister unless there's a crowd of friends around are really saying they don't care enough about their sibling to give any personal time or attention to the relationship.

The following story is about a woman who didn't know that crowds are not the place for personal bonding.

I have to stand in line to greet my sister

Just once, I'd like to be invited to my sister's home when she isn't having something that looks like a block party. My sister and I haven't said a word to each other in private for years. I never see her alone. I feel like an emotional pauper standing at the edge of a crowd watching the queen drive by. When I ask her for lunch, or just for a cup of tea, she always suggests that we include some- one else. I don't think she really knows anything about me personally or even wants to. I'm just another name in her address book.

Uncaring Siblings

Some sibling relationships have no give and take. A sibling who does all the talking and forgets to listen is like a thirsty deer who comes to a water hole and forgets to drink. Listening is another way of saying you care about a person.

The following story about a twin who forgot to listen shows how such people can never know the joy of a full and caring relationship.

My twin was once the other half of my heart

When we meet I ask my twin brother about his family, his health, his job, his concerns. He tells me in detail about each but never asks after me or mine in return. If I try to offer information, he interrupts me midsentence to add some detail about his own life. When I do get a word in he never hears what I'm saying. I think he is only trying to decide what he will elaborate on when I have finished talking.

Interfering Siblings

The opposite of uncaring is interfering. Some brothers and sisters, usually those born first, never seem to realize that their younger siblings are no longer children in need of guidance. Such people will intrude on their siblings' marriages, encroach on their decisions, pry into their finances, and even intercede for them during business decisions. Interfering siblings fail to recognize that their adult brothers and sisters have the right to their own privacy and even the right to make their own mistakes. Dominant siblings who subjugate weaker brothers or sisters to their will can never enjoy a loving relationship with them.

The following story shows how being a dominating sibling can cause a brother or sister to shut you out.

Now I do things behind my sister's back

When I was a child I looked to my older sister to tell me what to do. She, more than my parents who were both busy with their careers, ran my life. My sister told me what to wear, what friends I should cultivate, and what I should do in my spare time. She even decided what I should choose for my life's work. She told me to become a nurse, and I became a nurse. My sister still tries to run my life, but recently I've developed a will of my own. She gets angry when I make a decision without consulting her. To avoid her wrath I've taken to doing things behind her back. When she eventually finds out that I've done something about which she hasn't been consulted, I'm scolded like a small child.

User Siblings

It's safe to say that life is made up of a goodly portion of "sibling users" and a fairly equal portion of "sibling givers." Users seek out givers and take whatever they can get. Those who allow themselves to be used are often misguided, thinking they are doing their brother or sister a favor. In truth, constant and unquestioning givers only weaken a user's character another notch with each giving.

The following story illustrates how users can be losers when they finally forfeit their sibling's love.

I hear from my brother when he wants something

I know when I open a letter from my brother that the last paragraph will be a request for a favor. A lot of snow falls in the beginning paragraphs of any of his letters, but at the end the request always comes. Phone calls follow the same format. Two minutes of chatter and then the hit. Just once I wish my brother would write me or call me when he didn't want something.

Patronizing Siblings

Some siblings who think they are older, wiser, richer, and better looking, tend to patronize the siblings they see as less endowed. Such condescension tends to kill off true and honest communication. Siblings who are hollow flatterers, who speak in hypocritical tones and with insincere tongues may find they are not believed when they do come to their siblings with words of truth.

The following story shows how a hypocritical sibling may fool only herself.

Aren't you clever?

I wish I had a nickel for every time my sister has verbally patted me on the head and gushed some condescending phrase that is so far from the truth it leaves me feeling embarrassed for both of us. I don't want to be told that I look "beautiful" when I know it's one of my dowdy days. And I don't want to hear that my house is "charming" when my young sons have just trashed the decor with an impromptu game of cowboys. Just once if my sister were to say, "This place looks like a cyclone hit it," we might be able to laugh together with a new closeness.

Critical Siblings

Some people don't seem able to talk with their brothers and sisters without pointing out little faults and urging correction. Some are constantly in the act of passing judgment on their siblings' actions, censuring their conversations, and even attempting to analyze their thoughts. This is a sure way to condemn a closeness of feeling.

The following story is about a brother who left an indelible red mark on his relationship with his sibling.

I wrote him a letter and he sent it back corrected

I don't know that I have ever done anything that won my brother's total approval. I don't like to speak in his presence because he corrects my grammar and questions any facts I might present. I never write to him anymore. The last time I wrote him, which was several years ago, he sent my letter back with corrections for spelling and punctuation marked in red ink.

Name-Caller Siblings

Some people have to put a tag on everything and everybody, even their siblings. There are those who call their brothers and sisters things like:

- fatso,
- dummy,
- wimp,
- loud mouth.

Laughter may follow name-calling, but usually the person laughing isn't the one who was ridiculed.

This story is about a brother who was a sibling-relationship "illiterate."

My brother called me a computer illiterate

I'm not a computer wiz, in fact, just looking at a screen inhibits me. My brother talks in bytes, files, and commands. He shakes his head and looks down his nose at me when I don't understand what he is saying. This is just his grown-up way of making fun of me to build himself up. He's done this all our lives. He called me "Spelling Dummy" in grade school, the "Tin Man" when I got my braces in middle school, and "Lover Boy" when I couldn't get a date to the high-school prom. Now he calls me the "Computer Illiterate." Ever since I can remember my brother has tried to make himself look good by calling me names.

Two-Faced Siblings

Deceitful siblings who tell their brothers and sisters one thing to their face then another to the nearest listener are being hypocritical about loving their sibling. Real caring is based on truth.

The following story is about a sister who didn't know the truth about caring.

She was laughing behind my back

My sister told every one of us six brothers and sisters that we alone were her favorite sibling. When she thought I believed her I heard her tell her husband I was a "gullible sap." They both laughed, but I didn't stay to hear more. I don't need that kind of sister.

Jealous Siblings

Some people don't want to grow up; they don't want to make room for the marriage partners and children they think will come between them and their siblings. They want to keep their brothers and sisters for themselves alone and are jealous of anyone who tries to widen the circle of this relationship. Siblings can be special to one another always, even into old age. In real sibling closeness there is no room for jealousy.

The following story of a jealous maid of honor shows how such narrowness can strangle love.

She cried when I told her I was getting married

I was hoping my sister would be happy for me. I wanted her to be surprised when I told her I was engaged. Instead she burst into tears and said she didn't want to hear about wedding plans and she didn't want to be my maid of honor. I've

never been able to make my sister see that she
has a special place in my heart that no one can
replace. She refuses to believe that as we grow
older we need others in our lives, too. This kind
of jealous love strangles real feeling.

No one should be disheartened if the quotes just given
seem to parallel a few of their own sibling situations.
No relationship is perfect. Siblings are heir to their
share of differences and disagreements, too. But sibling problems, like all relationship problems, have
solutions. In the chapters that follow, all of the common denominators for poor sibling relationships will
be discussed, and practical answers to help remedy
these situations will be offered.

Chapter 5 in a Nutshell

No relationship is perfect. Kinships are heir to problems the same as any other type of relationship. Some
types of siblings who make kin caring difficult are:

- unreliable siblings,
- indifferent siblings,
- uncaring siblings,
- interfering siblings,
- user siblings,
- patronizing siblings,
- critical siblings,
- name-calling siblings,
- two-faced siblings,
- jealous siblings.

For every problem siblings can bring to a relationship, there is a solution. Practical answers follow.

6

Common Denominators: Good Sibling Relationships

No discussion of sibling relationships would be completely fair if only the faults were presented without a look at the happy and loving side of kin caring. The joys of having and being a sibling almost always outshine any drawbacks. To illustrate this truth the stories in this chapter are all about good sibling relationships and the positive factors that can contribute to this kind of kin caring.

A Basic Truth About Good Relationships

The word "caring" might best be used as the basic description of any good sibling relationship. Siblings who care listen to one another, help each other when trouble looms, are close when comfort is needed, back off and give space when a sibling wants to be alone, and even allow each other the privilege of making mistakes. Caring siblings take pride in the way they are alike as a family while they continue to respect that they are each different and unique.

Accepting Siblings

Accepting your brothers or sisters on the basis of what they are and not what you would like them to be is the foundation on which good sibling relationships are built. Good siblings don't try to make one another over, pepper their conversations with corrections, or ask favors and give none in return. Siblings should live by golden rules of conduct.

- Enjoy the ways your sibling is different from you and learn what you can from another viewpoint.
- Be glad your sibling isn't perfect. (If this were so, think how you would be outshone.)
- Overlook imperfections in your sibling and hope that you will be granted the same.

The story that follows is about a brother who lived by these rules.

My brother accepts me for what I am

My brother is always kind to me no matter how many times I tread on his toes. The other day I borrowed his new car and put a dent in the fender. When I came home and told him about it he didn't even get mad. He just asked me how it happened, and when he found out it wasn't my fault he told me not to worry. I want to be more like my brother. I hope I can learn from him to be patient and kind.

Forgiving Siblings

Some siblings resent childhood slights for years. Some hold grudges about simple and unintentional mistakes. People who have the grace to look beyond a brother's or sister's past weaknesses and errors leave the future open to a giving and loving relationship.

The following story is about a brother who had much to begrudge but never held onto bitter memories.

My brother is always willing to start over

I've hurt my brother more times than I care to think about. Starting as children, because I was bigger and stronger, I pushed him around. When the folks weren't looking I took his share of the goodies as well as mine. He didn't tattle or cry out. And although I don't want to, I'm still managing to hurt him. I was offered the job he wanted. His son ignored him and came to me when he wanted help. I'd hold a grudge about any one of these things, but not my brother. He's always ready to see the other side of the question.

Dependable Siblings

Being worthy of trust, being someone a sibling can rely on for support in a time of need, being a confidant who can listen and never tell—every brother and sister hopes to find all these attributes in their siblings.

This story illustrates how dependability says caring.

She's there when I need her

I phoned my sister in the middle of the night to ask for help. My car had run out of gas on the north freeway. Even while I was talking to her she was pulling on her shoes, trying to remember where she put the gas can, and planning to fix the thermos of hot coffee she would bring. I knew I could depend on her, that she was there for me, that she would come at my call.

Loving Siblings

A relationship between siblings who love one another
and are willing to show that love in words and deeds
can weather time and trouble.

Without awkwardness and embarrassment . . .

- siblings should express their feelings of love in
  words;
- siblings should reach out and embrace one another, demonstrating their love physically;
- siblings should rejoice in one another's good
  fortune;
- siblings should weep with one another in times
  of sorrow.

The story that follows shows how one brother ex-
pressed his love in many small ways.

My brother never forgets to tell me he loves me

When my brother says he loves me I know he's
not just mouthing idle words. He shows his love
in so many other ways. He calls me when I'm
sad and alone. Like the time my dog died, he came
over and stayed the whole afternoon. He writes
to me to tell me I'm important to him even though
we live in the same town. I got two letters of encouragement from him the week after I lost my first
job. It helped me to know he believed in me and
to see his expression of that belief in words. He
shares my joys too. When I got a new job he took
me to lunch. When I got a new puppy my brother
was the first one to send dog toys. These little
things he does are his other way of saying he
loves me.

Honest Siblings

When a sibling asks to hear the truth, that request should be honored without hedging. No double meanings, no flattery, no ambiguous expressions can replace the truth in honest relationships. Straightforward requests call for straightforward answers. How much better it is to hear the truth regarding one's weaknesses from someone you love than to hear from some unkind critic that you have been laughed at or left out.

The following story about a painful truth, asked of a brother, shows how a sibling needed honesty, not false flattery.

I needed to know the truth

My life was a sham. I'd told myself I was a dancer, that success was coming after the very next audition. I lived in a dream world, taking imaginary bows that would never come. I knew that only my brother would tell me the truth. I asked him for that truth and he saw the sincerity of my asking. He saw that it wasn't time to varnish the facts, it wasn't time for white lies. His honesty hurt for a time, but it hurt with love. The hurt is over and I've started a new life.

Open-Minded Siblings

Siblings who keep an open mind, who reserve their opinions, who are flexible in their outlook and willing to accept new ideas can lend a vision to their relationships with their brothers and sisters that will allow for ongoing growth and increasing closeness.

The following story illustrates how being an open-minded brother or sister can win a sibling's love.

She was always willing to accept the new me

Once or twice I tried to shock my sister into disapproval, but even my green hair didn't stop her embrace. I join all the oddball groups and take up all the far-out fads but my sister never sits in judgment on my lifestyle. Once I invited her to a protest march and she came. It wasn't easy for her mixing in my crowd, but she even told me afterward she'd learned something. I love her because she's always willing to take me for what I am.

Generous Siblings

The siblings who give more than they take, leave the door open to a happy and generous relationship in return.

Siblings should be willing to give their time to help, to listen, to admire, and to love their brothers and sisters. It is often the busy sibling who finds time to spare.

Siblings should be willing to give generously of what they have, to share worldly goods with their brothers and sisters. It is often siblings who have little to spare who give much, even to the point of depriving themselves.

Siblings should strive to stay aware of their brother's and sister's needs and give of themselves before being asked. The following story is of such generous sibling insight.

He gave me all four apples

My brother and I were out of work, and so we went out each day to find something we could do to bring home money to feed our children. It was a desperate time and sometimes the day's end saw us empty-handed. On one such day when I had found no work, I met my brother as I was going home. My pockets were empty. My brother was smiling and carrying a large sack. When I asked him what he carried he said he had been given some apples by a neighbor. Looking at my sad face he realized no one had offered me anything that day. Reaching into the sack, one by one, he took out four apples and put them into my baggy coat pockets. What I didn't know, until the neighbor told me many days later, was that four apples were all the large sack had contained. He had given me everything without even letting me know.

If some of the quotes just given sounded like thoughts you have shared with your siblings, be grateful for the warm and loving spirit of your relationships. Hold onto these positive thoughts and learn to build on them.

Chapter 6 in a Nutshell

Caring is the basis for a good and loving sibling relationship. Siblings who care about one another are:

- accepting of faults,
- forgiving of errors,
- dependable when needed,
- loving,
- open-minded,
- generous and giving.

Learn to build on the positive aspects of your relationship with your sibling.

7

Look at Your Past Sibling Relationships

If you are sincere in your desire to rebuild new relationships with your siblings, you would do well to begin this renewal by reconsidering your past associations with them to determine how that past may affect the future.

- Were your childhood sibling ties unhappy?
- Were your childhood sibling ties loving and close?

In this chapter you are asked to take a look at your early sibling struggles and your childhood hours of harmony. Both the good and the bad things that you discover about these early days will make useful tools for bettering your future.

- When you uncover what was bitter about the past you have the basis for changing and improving the days to come.
- When you uncover what was happy about the past you have the blocks on which to build further successes.

You may be in for some surprises when you begin to uncover feelings long buried. If these feelings are resentful, best they are uncovered and finally forgiven or resolved. If you had good rapport with one or more of your siblings, you will enjoy this journey through those happy memories and want to build new memories to match the old ones.

The groups of questions that follow are not meant to be tests. There is no failing or passing grade at the end. Both sympathetic and contentious questions are posed to give you an idea of how your past feelings shape and influence your present attitudes. Your answers to the questions will be tools to help you attain better sibling relationships in the future.

Questions are short and straightforward and are not designed to be pondered over at length in search of gray areas. Try not to weigh too many factors in coming to a conclusion. Reply to each question spontaneously. Accept the answer that comes off the top of your head as your first emotions register. Consider only your own feelings, not those of your siblings. Run through the questions with only *one* sibling in mind. Repeat the questions to analyze your past relationship with each additional sibling. Your answers will help you decide:

- whether you had a past relationship with your siblings that was warm and loving,
- whether you had a past relationship with your siblings that was belligerent and harmful,
- whether you were so indifferent to your siblings you have little left of a relationship at all,
- whether others strongly influenced your thinking and feelings about your siblings.

Were You and Your Siblings Good to Each Other?

Your answers to the questions that follow will help you determine whether your childhood sibling relationships were happy and giving. Siblings who loved each other often showed this love in many outward ways.

Questions: Answer "True" or "False" for each question.

1. You and your sibling confided in each other.

    _____ True   _____ False

2. You and your sibling protected one another from belligerent outsiders.

    _____ True   _____ False

3. You wanted to look and act like your sibling.

    _____ True   _____ False

4. Most of the time you could tell your sibling's mood without asking.

    _____ True   _____ False

5. You did not like to be apart from your sibling for long periods of time.

    _____ True   _____ False

6. When things went well for your sibling you were happy about this.

    _____ True   _____ False

7. You often shared treats and gifts with your sibling.

_____ True   _____ False

8. When your sibling was sad you tried to be of comfort.

_____ True   _____ False

9. You tried to help your sibling reach hoped-for goals.

_____ True   _____ False

10. You planned to stay close to your sibling always.

_____ True   _____ False

Analysis: Use the following analysis to determine if your past feelings for your sibling were loving and giving.

10 "True" answers: You and your sibling had a genuine regard for each other's feelings. You have an excellent basis for renewed relationships.

7 or 8 "True" answers: You and your sibling will need to work at relationship renewal, but your efforts have a good chance of succeeding.

6 or fewer "True" answers: You and your sibling had problems relating to each other in the past, and you will need to guard against falling into old patterns.

Were You and Your Sibling Bad to Each Other?

Your answers to the questions that follow will help you determine whether your childhood sibling relationships were hurtful and repressive.

Questions: Select one answer for each question.

1. How would you describe your emotions when you learned that your sibling received a favor and you did not?

   (A) _____ anger and jealousy
   (B) _____ indifference
   (C) _____ glad for the sibling

2. What action did you take when you found out your sibling was doing something forbidden?

   (A) _____ ran and tattled
   (B) _____ stayed indifferent
   (C) _____ promised not to tell

3. When someone praised your sibling in your presence, what was your reaction?

   (A) _____ stepped in and tried to grab the limelight
   (B) _____ wanted to put my sibling down
   (C) _____ agreed with praise

4. What did you do when you were asked to go somewhere with your sibling?

   (A) _____ refused to go
   (B) _____ took my sibling and then made the outing an unpleasant one
   (C) _____ went and enjoyed my sibling's company

5. Did you give gifts to your sibling on birthdays?

   (A) _____ never
   (B) _____ only if my sibling had given me one
   (C) _____ yes

6. Did you approve of your sibling's appearance?

   (A) _____ no
   (B) _____ sometimes made negative remarks
   (C) _____ admired my sibling's appearance

7. Did you ever do little favors for your sibling without being asked?

   (A) _____ never
   (B) _____ if I wanted something in return
   (C) _____ yes

8. What did you do when something embarrassing happened to your sibling?

   (A) _____ laughed with others and enjoyed my sibling's predicament
   (B) _____ kept quiet and was glad it wasn't me
   (C) _____ tried to comfort my sibling

9. Did you ever express love for your sibling?

   (A) _____ never
   (B) _____ only when my sibling spoke first
   (C) _____ often

10. How would you best describe your sibling as a child?

   (A) _____ a mean little brat
   (B) _____ someone I wanted to avoid
   (C) _____ a good friend

Analysis: Use the following analysis to determine if your past sibling relationships were destructive.

1. For every "A" answer give yourself 2 negative points.

2. For every "B" answer give yourself 1 negative point.

3. For every "C" answer give yourself 1 "relationship hopeful" point.

More than 10 negative points: You were a poor sibling and you probably know it. You are going to have to work very hard to overcome the damage you have done to your relationship in the past.

Between 5 and 8 negative points: You were a rather indifferent sibling in the past. You will need to prove yourself to your sibling before a new basis of confidence can be established.

For every "C" answer: Your relationship renewal becomes more hopeful with every "C" answer. More than two "C's" and your task of relationship renewal will be light.

Were You and Your Sibling Indifferent to Each Other?

Maybe you had almost no relationship with your sibling in the past. Maybe each family member went separate and uncaring ways. These questions will tell you if you damaged your future sibling relationships by indifference.

Questions: Answer either "Yes" or "No" to each question.

1. I knew my sibling's favorite color.

_____ Yes   _____ No

2. I knew my sibling's favorite food.

_____ Yes   _____ No

3. I knew my sibling's goals and ambitions.

_____ Yes   _____ No

4. I could tell when my sibling was depressed without having to be told.

_____ Yes   _____ No

5. I often asked my sibling to go places with me.

_____ Yes   _____ No

6. I took time to listen to my sibling.

_____ Yes   _____ No

7. I knew my sibling's friends.

_____ Yes   _____ No

8. I came to my sibling's aid when help was needed.

_____ Yes   _____ No

9. I can remember at least three happy occasions I shared with my sibling.

_____ Yes   _____ No

10. When we were grown and had left the family home, my sibling and I kept in contact.

_____ Yes   _____ No

Analysis: Use the following analysis to determine if your past sibling relationships were indifferent.

8 to 10 "No" answers: You hardly knew your sibling was alive. Making amends will mean convincing your sibling that you are sincere.

7 to 4 "No" answers: You will have an uphill climb to convince your sibling you are interested in a relationship. The word renew is out of place as you didn't have much of a relationship to start with.

3 to 0 "No" answers: You are still probably in touch with your sibling. You may have had human failings but were a pretty good sibling right from the start.

Did Others Influence Your Sibling Relationships?

This section is designed to help you decide how much your family, your friends, or other contacts helped to shape your relationships with your siblings. How other people felt about your sibling could have made you proud, jealous, or even hateful.

Questions: Fill in the word or words that would be most fitting in each of the following situations.

    1. Mother loved my sibling _____ me.

        (A) better than
        (B) about the same
        (C) less than

    2. My friends _____ my sibling.

        (A) preferred
        (B) paid no attention to
        (C) disliked

3. My other relatives favored ____ .

(A) me
(B) neither of us
(C) my sibling

4. When something went wrong my parents blamed ____ .

(A) me
(B) neither or both of us
(C) my sibling

5. My friends and relatives gave gifts to ____ .

(A) my sibling
(B) neither or both of us
(C) me

6. People ____ said my sibling was better looking.

(A) often
(B) sometimes
(C) never

Analysis: Use the following analysis to determine if your past sibling relationships were influenced by others.

If you chose (A) on any of the questions, indicating things went in your sibling's favor, you were undoubtedly influenced by this action and may have resented your sibling's good fortune.

If you chose (B) on any of the questions, this indicates that others had little influence on your sibling relationships in this area.

If you chose (C) on any of the questions, where the action was in your favor, you may have come out best in that situation, but your sibling may resent you.

Keys to the Past

The sets of questions you have just asked yourself are meant to prompt your memory to summon up past feelings about your sibling relationships. There is no pass or fail grade for this quiz. The only failure will be if you decline to act on what you have learned.

Where you found *weakness and resentment* in your past relationships, strive to overcome these problems. Begin by reassuring your sibling that mistakes of the past will not be repeated.

Where you found *strengths and kindnesses* in your past relationships, strive to build on them to improve future bonds between you and your sibling.

Chapter 7 in a Nutshell

Your past relationships with your siblings may have been influenced for the good or harmed by . . .

- you and your sibling,
- your family,
- your friends and acquaintances,
- total strangers.

A look at your past relationships with your siblings can tell you where a renewal of kin caring may mean changing your ways to correct past mistakes, or where the strengths of the past are there to build on in the future.

8

Look at Your Present Sibling Relationships

Many people lead lives so crowded with pressing daily needs, they seldom pause to think about their siblings. Brothers and sisters are those people that there will be time for tomorrow. Often, however, that tomorrow with time for siblings just doesn't happen. If you are one of those procrastinating siblings, or if you're just not sure how much time you do give to kin caring, this chapter will help you explore the frequency and quality of your current sibling contacts.

Fill in the blanks in the questions that follow and you will see for yourself just where your relationships with your siblings stand. Bring your memory up to date on how much caring you have given your kin in the last few weeks. You need not dig back too far into your memory. A week or two will tell you all you need to know about the flow and flavor of your give-and-take relationships.

Answer questions without qualifying your answers. Run through the questions with only *one* sibling in mind. Repeat the questions for other siblings.

No scores need be tallied, and no grades will be given. When you have finished answering the questions, you will know what kind of sibling relationships you have without needing to add up credits or debits.

Closeness Quiz

Unless you keep a calendar and mark off each time your sibling calls and you return a call, or you record each time you write a letter or receive one, time has a way of slipping past and good intentions never get acted upon. To get a focus on your recent actions regarding your sibling, answer "Yes" or No" to each of the following.

In the Past Month . . .

1. I have visited my sibling.

   Yes _____   No _____

   If your sibling lives close by and you haven't visited, your "No" answer is all the more damning. Two sisters who live in a duplex often tap hello on their adjoining wall. The taps, they say, are like visits without intrusion.

2. I have telephoned my sibling.

   Yes _____   No _____

   If you wait until you want something or have bad news to relate before you call your sibling, your call doesn't count as a loving gesture. One sister who calls her elderly brother each week makes a list of good things to tell him. She tries to get him to at least chuckle before she ends their telephone conversation.

3. I have written to my sibling.

   Yes _____   No _____

   Even if you live next door, personal, caring messages can mean a lot to your sibling. No need to wait for special occasions. One brother who used to write his sister only on her birthday, now writes on that date every month. She says it is like having the joy and not the aging of twelve birthday celebrations.

4. I have said something good about my sibling.

Yes _____   No _____

People don't need to know your siblings to hear good things about them. Praising your siblings strengthens your love for them. Putting your siblings down to others destroys love. One brother who constantly told his friends what a great nurse his sister was found that his praise was responsible for her receiving a new job offer.

5. I have sent my sibling a gift.

Yes _____   No _____

Small, inexpensive gifts, sent regularly and for no special reason, are worth more than lavish presents doled out for a few landmark events. One brother who knows his sister likes to garden, drops by with a six-pack of bedding plants once every month. She is reminded of his love when the gift is given and many times over as the flowers bloom.

6. I have sent my siblings snapshots.

Yes _____   No _____

Even if you see your sibling frequently, sending photos of happy events is a way of sharing those times and drawing closer together. You don't have to be an accomplished photographer to share photos. Members of a California family, who don't mind laughing at themselves, have started an ongoing "Poor Photography Contest" to share blurry, headless, overexposed, and unidentifiable photos. They share a new family closeness, too.

In Contacting My Sibling . . .

It should not be considered a quality contact if you call or go to see your sibling only to complain, give bad news, ask a favor, brag about something you've done, or remind them of mistakes they've made. A contact should be for showing interest, expressing love, and hearing about how your sibling is doing.

To measure the quality of your recent sibling contacts, either by phone or in person, answer "Yes" or "No" to each of the following.

1. I ask about my sibling's health.

Yes _____   No _____

Being concerned about your sibling's mental and physical health is another way of saying you care. Some ways of asking health questions might include:

- How have you been sleeping lately?
- Has your appetite been good?
- Do you get out for your daily exercise?

2. I listen to my sibling's concerns.

Yes _____   No _____

Listening to your sibling is the key to building strong relationships that time cannot erode. When your sibling has worries, you should encourage discussion about the roots of those worries. Sometimes problems can talk themselves out.

3. I share my sibling's joys.

Yes _____   No _____

Half the joy of winning is having someone to share in the victory. Recognize your sibling's joy and you increase it. Whether it is a tennis match, a bingo game, or a new job, when your sibling makes a gain, recognize the accomplishment with praise and celebration.

4. I extend invitations to my sibling.

Yes _____   No _____

Giving of yourself, sharing your time, is the most important gift you can give your sibling. A paper cup of hot coffee shared as you sit on a park bench is giving. An invitation to take in a department-store sale together is giving. Don't wait to ask your sibling to an expensive outing. Small outings that come frequently say more than costly ones.

5. I offer to do things for my sibling.

Yes _____   No _____

Just going to the store, mailing a letter, or replacing an out-of-reach light bulb can say you care. Some ideas for helping out are:

- tax form help,
- transportation to and from an airport,
- pet care,
- plant watering.

The deed done without being asked is twice as sweet as carrying out a request.

6. I tell my sibling of my love.

Yes _____   No _____

Don't wait for an occasion to say "I love you." Say it soon and often. Say "I love you and thank you" when your sibling does something for you. Say "I love you" as you end a phone conversation. Say "I love you" at the close of a letter. Say it when you enjoy a good laugh or when you cry together. "I love you" are words that never grow old and can never be said too often when the words are sincere.

Analysis: Your answers will tell you what kind of sibling relationship you have today.

If the number of "No" answers outweighs the positive replies, you have allowed caring to erode.

If you were able to say "Yes" to many of the questions, you and your sibling have a solid core of shared love that you have helped to nurture.

From Your Sibling's Eyes

How would your sibling describe you? Honestly and basically, what words would your sibling use to portray your bonds of union? Does your sibling see you as a friend? Do you and your siblings trust one another and have a close affinity for one another? Try the word selection study that follows to theorize how your sibling might portray you.

Choose a word from either column A or column B that you think best describes the way your sibling sees you. Choose the first word that rings true, without pondering the different arguments that could be developed for each side of the question.

column A	column B
Generous	Stingy
Modest	Vain
Caring	Indifferent
Joyful	Complaining
Easygoing	Malcontent
Staid	Excitable
Witty	Monotonous
Friendly	Hostile
Courteous	Impolite
Warm-hearted	Spiteful
Grateful	Selfish
Forgiving	Vindictive
Trusting	Jealous

Analysis: If you circled words in column A more often than those in column B, you are probably a good sibling. Keep up your efforts and continue to enjoy your relationships.

If you circled the words in column B more often, you are going to have to work hard to build some better relationships. A less than perfect start doesn't mean you should give up on the idea of renewed closeness. Use what you have learned to make improvements. Keep a bookmark in this chapter and check yourself from time to time to see if you can improve your care rating.

Chapter 8 in a Nutshell

Explore the frequency and quality of your day-to-day contacts with your siblings. Ask yourself if you . . .

- visit,
- telephone,
- write,
- say good things about your sibling,
- give gifts,
- send pictures,

- ask about your sibling's health,
- listen to concerns,
- invite your sibling out,
- offer to help,
- tell of your love.

Take an honest look at yourself from your sibling's eyes.

Keep repeating the questions asked in this chapter to help yourself improve your care rating.

9

Get Your Head Ready

If the information you have read in the preceding chapters has left you with the feeling that your sibling relationships may have eroded with passing years or that they weren't all that good to start with, don't be discouraged. Recognizing the inadequacies of your past relationships with your siblings and knowing that you have to make changes should make you hopeful, not downcast. It is common for adult siblings to grow apart. The years that have passed since you left home and the miles between you lead to this.

Sibling relationships are vulnerable to stress from other outside sources as well. Parents can contribute to sibling differences and separation even among their adult children. A spouse, a friend, or a neighbor can drive a wedge between brothers and sisters. The secret to overcoming these difficulties often lies in the attitude adopted toward making changes for the better. When you recognize the need to change and admit the desire to come closer to your brothers and sisters, you have adopted the positive attitude that is the first step toward solution.

The suggestions that follow will help you support this positive attitude and add strength to your resolution to come closer to your siblings. Some of the suggestions are simple reminders to discontinue destructive habits. Others are reinforcements to bolster your efforts and support your morale.

Recognize Your Faults

Be willing to admit that you may be part of the reason you and your sibling are no longer close. Maybe your sibling has been wanting to be closer to you, has phoned, written, and come to see you, but you have been indifferent to these attempts at relationship renewal. Put the blame where it belongs, even if it's in your own backyard. Recognize that you are not always the perfect sibling.

Here is the story of a sibling who was almost too late discovering that his thoughtlessness was the reason his brother found it hard to love him.

> My brother said I intimidated him. This took me by surprise, but it also got me to thinking about how I treated my brother. I gave myself a mental playback of our last meeting. I'd tried to give him a stock market tip he didn't want. I'd suggested he try my barber for a better haircut. I'd even tried to tell him what to select from the lunch menu. No wonder he'd declined to meet me for lunch the following week.

Believe Change Is Possible

Pessimism has no place in a plan for change. Forget past problems. Forget that you may have tried to renew your sibling relationships before and failed. Now is the time to tell yourself that you can start over, and this time you can succeed.

Here is the story of a sibling who refused to give up on her attempts to renew her relationship with her unresponsive sister. When everything she tried failed to get a response, instead of getting angry, she used humor.

I wrote my sister every week for seven weeks. She didn't send me as much as a postcard. I called my sister twice a month for three months. She always seemed glad to hear my voice but she never called me back. Then one day I stuffed a note in an envelope and fired it off to her. The note had only one line, it said, "At the elbow!" Sure enough, my sister called when she received the message. She wanted to know what I meant, so I told her, "It means that if you don't write me or pick up the phone to call me I'm going to break your arm off at the elbow." It worked. We both laughed and she said from now on I could count on our relationship being one of both give and take.

Unlearn Bad Habits

Recognize the bad habits that eroded your sibling relationships in the first place and make a concerted effort to turn these habits around.

- If you have been critical of your sibing in the past, learn to seek out your sibling's good qualities and dwell on them.
- If you have been lazy about responding to your sibling's gestures of friendship, become the active one in renewed friendship efforts. Let your actions show that you are sincere about a new togetherness.
- If you have been late habitually when meeting your sibling, learn to arrive at appointments in advance of the stated time.
- If you have never let go of your cut-and-dried routines, learn to be more flexible about your sibling contacts.
- If you have been embarrassed to show your affection, to reach out to your sibling and say, "I love you," practice up and use the words often.

Turning your bad habits around can lead to a little turning by your sibling as well. Praise, love, respect, and interest are all contagious. Start some new habits and make them good ones.

Here is the story of two brothers who licked one bad habit they shared.

Both Ned and I like to drink a little beer, but sometimes our drinking led us into a critical vein with one another. We never got this way when we drank with friends, just with one another. I drank a beer and told my brother he was getting fat. He drank a beer and told me I'd been at my old job too long. First thing we knew what had begun as a happy evening ended in a quarrel. One morning after a particularly bitter argument we agreed that when we got together we would never drink anything stronger than coffee. Now we are friends.

Bury Old Grudges

It is necessary to stop hating before you can begin to love. Brooding over the past is wasting time. Determine what can be done to prevent old problems from recurring and take positive steps to carry out your plans. Forgive yourself and your siblings for errors made yesterday and get on with tomorrow.

- Never mind if mother loved him best.
- Forget that you had to wear hand-me-down dresses.
- Pardon things said in anger.
- Bury the old slights and wounds you thought would never heal.

Old grudges, like worn-out shoes, should be tossed aside and forgotten. Left-over bitterness should have no place in your new, loving relationships.

Set Goals and Make Plans

Just as you wouldn't start on any important journey without charting your route, you shouldn't count on happy future relations with your siblings without laying out some kind of plan or set of goals that point toward what you hope the future will be like.

Any plan for a renewed sibling relationship would do well to include the following suggestions. (Note: These are only suggestions, meant to be used or rejected as pattern and opportunity present themselves.)

1. *Decide which sibling you will approach first.* Concentrate on renewing a relationship with only one brother or sister at a time. Show that one sibling you care. Work to improve that one relationship before you go on to another. Staging a big family reunion will not offer the personal approach needed for new and better communication with any one sibling. First, make one special sibling the core of your caring.

2. *Decide what action you will take to make your first gesture of renewal.* A first contact may be something as simple as a phone call, a short visit, or a long-overdue letter. Expect your sibling to be a little wary and questioning if you haven't made contact in a long time. Explain why you have surfaced. In simple terms, admit neglect and say you hope to do better in the future. Honest communication should lead the way back to better days.

3. *Plan the timing of your first contact.* Make your first contact at a time that is convenient for your sibling. Calling or dropping in when you know your sister is busy getting dinner or putting her twins to bed, or when you know she may be rushing off to work is not good timing. Make it easy for your sibling to relax and enjoy a contact with you. Pick a time when it will be possible for your sibling to meet your gesture halfway.

4. *Plan what you are going to say when you make your first contact.* Planning what you are going to

say does not mean constructing word-for-word conversations. You can be in trouble with this agenda when the first reply differs from your outline. Planning means you should try to think of positive things to say or write to your sibling. Build on the good memories you have together. Ask your sibling a question and be genuine about your interest in the reply. Do more listening or asking than talking or reporting. Remember what your sibling tells you and build on that information in your next questions and replies.

5. *Know what your second step will be before you begin with the first step.* Plan ahead. Set goals for the first month, the first six months, and the first year of your renewed contact. Think beyond your first call, your first visit, your first letter. Make plans for ongoing contacts. Promise your sibling you will call or write on a regular basis. Follow through on this promise and calendar upcoming contacts. If schedules have to be adjusted, tell your sibling and then make changes, but don't discontinue your efforts when all that is needed is a little flexibility.

Take Action

Just talking about, thinking about, and making elaborate plans to contact your sibling will never get you any closer to your goals. For any results to come about you must actually put your foot out and take that first step. Do something. Take some action.

The following story illustrates the futility of planning when no action is taken.

There were two things I was always saying I was going to do. I was going to get together with my sister and I was going to write a book. I made plans in my head. I would take my sister to lunch. I gave my imagined book different titles. I fantasized about what a good time my sister and I would have and about how I was going to spend all the money my book made. I didn't call my sister and I never put a line of my book on paper. One day I sat down and figured out that if I had written one page for every day I had planned to write, over the years I could have produced a full set of encyclopedia. That was the shock that made me decide to change. I haven't written a book, but I've put a stop to planning in my head. The day after I added up my imaginary pages I called my sister. I don't just plan imaginary visits to my sister anymore. I see her often now.

Be Realistic About Progress

In any situation where change is necessary, you need to recognize that trying something new sometimes means failing. Defeat should be your signal to try again. Old habits that have become ingrained and old grudges that have accumulated over the years cannot be swept away in a few days. Even when both you and your sibling vow to change, one, the other, or both of you may fall back into old ways and repeat past mistakes. Expect progress to be slow and you will not become discouraged. Be unwilling to give up on trying even if your first attempts to begin anew are rejected. One sandbag can't stop a flood. One phone call won't establish a new relationship. Be willing and ready to try again and again to reach your sibling with acts, deeds, and words of caring.

A Brief Attitude Quiz

If the suggestions just outlined seem like they will involve too much commitment, your attitude needs work. You can't expect success if you aren't willing to give of yourself on a repeat basis. Ask yourself—

"Do I really want a better and closer relationship with my sibling?" If your answer is "Yes," then learn to accept that such closeness is going to take time and effort. Nothing worthwhile is ever accomplished without some doing. Reward is often directly connected to effort.

Chapter 9 in a Nutshell

When you recognize the inadequacies of your relationships with your sibling and admit the need for change, you have taken the first positive steps toward renewed kin caring.

Suggestions to help relationship renewals:

- recognize your faults,
- believe change is possible,
- unlearn bad habits,
- bury old grudges,
- set goals and make plans,
- take action,
- don't give up.

A change for the better will take effort on your part. Your reward is often directly connected to that effort.

10

Suggestions That Work
and Pitfalls to Avoid

Several suggestions for a successful reconciliation with your sibling follow in this chapter. Also included are pitfalls to avoid if you ever want to hear from that sibling again. While these suggestions may help to smooth your progress, they should be adapted to your individual situation and taken with this additional word of advice.

- No suggestion is workable for all people in all situations.
- Pitfalls for some people may be workable ideas for others.

Reconciliation Suggestions for Success

Other people's suggestions may help you along the way toward reconciliation, but any new closeness you derive from these ideas depends, in large measure, upon your willingness to commit time and interest to your efforts. Just reading the ideas that follow will not lead to a successful reconciliation. You must provide the initiative and energy needed to put the suggestions into motion.

In general it is best if your approach is a quiet one. Your actions should indicate you aren't trying to make a grand and sweeping impression, simply a sincere one.

Here first are success suggestions. They may be of some help to you. Good luck.

Phone First

If you haven't been in contact with your sibling for a long period of time, don't plan a surprise visit or drop a chatty letter in the mail. Before you make any other approach, telephone your sibling and be honest about why you are calling. Admit neglect. Express interest in renewed closeness. If your sibling is cool, be willing to go more than halfway. Eat humble pie. Gentle opening gestures say you are sincere.

Show Interest

You have some catching up to do so try to find out about your sibling's current interests. Ask about your sibling's health. Show an interest in your sibling's work or family. Ask general, not too personal, questions and listen carefully to the replies. This is the information that can have a definite bearing on your future relationship together.

- If you learn that your sibling is in poor health, this may open up opportunities for you to be helpful.
- If you learn that your sibling is an extremely busy person, this may limit the amount of time you can give to each other.

Asking questions and listening to replies is a very important part of building relationships.

Send a Reminder of Past Pleasures

Hooking onto the coattail of a happy childhood is a good way to begin a reconciliation as adults. Try to think of reminders of the past that you can share with your sibling. Maybe you sang together as children. Send your sibling a book about singing. Maybe you still have an old photograph or two of your childhood days. Share a snapshot. Don't make the gesture a grand and sweeping one—just offer the gift simply and quietly.

- One sister sent her sibling crocheted pot holders from a pattern they used as children.
- One brother sent his sibling a tiny model car like the first car they owned together.

Extend an Invitation

Invite your sibling to have lunch, to visit you, to take a trip to the mountains or the seashore. Make the invitation easy to accept. Go to your sibling's territory; don't expect your sibling to travel to yours. Don't make a big deal out of the fact you are picking up the tab for an outing. Make your invitation a casual one. Start out small, with a simple outing at first. You can always do something on a grander scale later, after a few successes.

Send a Gift Without Waiting for an Occasion

Share a book you have enjoyed, send candy, buy a puzzle and solve it halfway. This first gift should be a small, simple gesture. Remember, you are tiptoeing into your sibling's life again. Big bouquets of flowers or expensive and ostentatious gifts can come across as pompous.

Ask Whether You May Visit

Invite yourself for a visit to your sibling's home, but be sensitive to the reaction you receive. Listen for acceptance, hesitancy, or resignation in the reply and let that be your lead. Visit only at an appointed time, one that is convenient for your sibling. If you live nearby, make your first visit a short one. If you must come a long way, stay no longer than two days, especially if you are putting someone out of a bed. Be a quiet guest who slips into the household routine and helps with the chores.

Bring a Visitor's Gift

Never come on a visit with empty hands, even if you only come for the afternoon. Make your gift a simple one, perhaps something with a tie to the past. A basket of your sibling's favorite fruit or a bag of the kind of candy you enjoyed as children can say you are remembering happy times together.

Help with Problems

Don't make your sibling ask you for help. If your brother or sister is sick, has lost a job, or been in an accident, be there and be helpful. Don't excuse yourself by saying you'd just be in the way. Find an unobtrusive, quiet way to be useful. For example:

- drive your sibling's children to appointments,
- do the grocery shopping and tuck in a little treat or two at your own expense,
- pick up a couple of magazines.

Make your usefulness fit into your sibling's routine.

Remind Your Sibling of the World's Beauty

There could be no finer way to say you care than to give your sibling a tangible piece of the world's beauty. There are so many ways to do this.

- Send a beautiful piece of music.
- Send a photograph of a sunset.
- Send the first spring flowers.
- Give a basket full of red apples.
- Send a jar of smooth stones glistening with water.
- Give an old leather book of favorite poetry.

Beauty is always something your sibling can enjoy no matter how busy, bored, or unhappy. Beauty has a way of turning life into a wonder.

Make Your Sibling Laugh

If you last parted in anger or disagreement, reconciliation may be too emotional to be looked at straight. Try to approach your sibling from a different angle with no mention of the past. The different angle could be humor.

Maybe one of the following ideas can help you laugh together and forget the past.

- Dress in a silly costume when you visit.
- Hire a tuba player to come with you and play your sibling's favorite song.
- Fill a shopping bag with dandelion blossoms and dump them at your sibling's feet.
- Try out an old gag.
- Give a rubber chicken.

Remember, never laugh at, but always laugh with your sibling. If someone has to be the butt of the joke, let it be you. Be the straight man in a two-way act, and let your sibling enjoy being the center of attention.

Reconciliation Pitfalls

Some gestures and actions can be reconciliation pitfalls. To avoid false starts and stumbles, these actions should be avoided.

Don't Boss Your Sibling

Even if you are an older sibling and were responsible for helping your brother or sister make decisions during childhood years, unlearn this habit. Adult siblings have the right to make their own decisions. Ask a question, then stand back and wait for the answer.

Don't Brag

Find positive things to say about your sibling's home, family, job, and progress. Don't brag about what you are doing or what you have to try to outshine your sibling's fortune.

Don't Lay Guilt Trips

Never try to force your sibling to visit you, write to you, or phone you by making sighing sounds and "don't mind me" statements. Reconciliation will be successful only if your sibling acts out of willingness to be close to you, not just to please you or because of undue pressure.

Don't Complain

Never mind reciting a litany of problems, reading off a list of the latest deaths, or crying on your sibling's shoulder because you are depressed and unhappy. Bring your good news and your joys to your sibling. When your voice is heard at the other end of the phone, don't let your sibling's first thought be, "What's happened now?"

Don't Tell Secrets

Even if a sibling doesn't say, "This is confidential," treat what you are told as something said in trust. When a sibling confides bad news, that information may not be intended for circulation to friends or to the rest of the family. When a sibling reports good fortune, let him or her be the one to have the pleasure of telling others the news.

Don't Pry

Some people are more open about their lives than others. If your brother or sister is reserved, respect his or her need to keep personal things private. Don't ask leading questions about domestic problems, lack of love life, or financial failures, and don't try to squeeze out personal information that is not offered willingly.

Don't Plan Too Much Togetherness

Both you and your sibling have another adult life to live now. You can't go back to the nest of closeness and live in one another's pocket again. Be glad for some renewed harmony, but don't move in on top of your sibling. Too much togetherness can lead to arguments and an eventual drifting apart.

Free Fall

The above suggestions are meant to be "words to the wise." No rule is without it's exception. You alone can determine what will work for you and your sibling. Your course of action must be absolutely unique, designed to fit the two of you alone. Take one step at a time and remember that success can't be rushed.

Chapter 10 in a Nutshell

Reconciliation Ideas That Work

- Make your first contact a phone call.
- Show interest in your sibling.
- Send a reminder of past pleasures.
- Extend an invitation.
- Send a gift without waiting for an occasion.
- Ask whether you may visit.
- When you visit, bring a gift.
- Be helpful if your sibling has a problem.
- Remind your sibling of the world's beauty.
- Make your sibling laugh.

Reconciliation Pitfalls

- Don't boss.
- Don't brag.
- Don't lay guilt trips.
- Don't complain.
- Don't tell your sibling's secrets to others.
- Don't pry.
- Don't plan too much togetherness.

11

Do You Communicate Like a Cat or a Dog?

This chapter is all about communication and its importance in your effort to renew sibling closeness.

Establishing good communication between you and your sibling is vital to the advance of any plan you may have for renewed closeness. However good your intentions and however well you have laid your plans, they can come to nothing if you do not communicate your feelings and your intentions. You can reach out, wanting to become close, but for lack of the right words fail to make your feelings known. Even when you are successful in conveying your own thoughts, if you do not listen for your sibling's reaction, you do not have two-way communication. Without an interchange of thoughts there can be no renewed relationship. A renewal of kin caring, to a great extent, depends upon how well you express your feelings and how well you listen to your sibling's replies.

In this chapter both good and bad communicators will be discussed. To illustrate these opposites, a cat will play the part of a poor communicator and a dog will portray a good communicator.

The Case of the Self-Centered Cat

In the example that follows, a cat, a very poor communicator, is featured. Each communication rule the cat breaks is named in an italicized statement preceding a narrative paragraph. Ask yourself if you treat your sibling like this cat treats its owner.

She failed to acknowledge my presence

I let myself in the front door and dropped my wet umbrella in the hall. It was warm in the house, and quiet. I was glad to be home. It had been a less than happy day. I'd made a critical mistake in my work at the office and my boss was pretty upset about it. To top that off I'd missed my bus by a few seconds and had to wait twenty minutes in the pouring rain for the next one.

I hung up my wet coat, kicked off my shoes, and went to the living room just to sit and do nothing for awhile. I flopped down on the couch with a sigh and looked blankly at the opposite wall for a minute, then my eyes focused on Ginger, our fat and sleek tabby cat. She was perched in her favorite spot atop the bookcase. Sensing my stare, she pretended to wake that very moment and notice me for the first time. I knew from experience that her hearing was excellent. From three rooms away she could detect a can of cat food being lifted from a kitchen shelf. She had probably been aware of my coming long before I'd put my key in the lock. But, of course, it might make her look interested or even eager if she did anything as friendly as coming to greet me. Even now she yawned twice and stretched elaborately instead of looking in my direction. Next, she busied herself by grooming her already shining coat. I began to speak to her as she licked herself. She continued to ignore me.

She failed to acknowledge me when I spoke to her

"It's been a punk day, Ginger," I appealed to her by name. "I could use a little companionship." Without so much as a flick of her whiskers in my direction, she finished cleaning her hind feet and began on her front paws. I spoke to her again. "Why don't you come over here and be of some comfort?" Her yellow eyes narrowed as she looked out the window, pretending to watch the rain. My invitation was ignored.

She changed the subject to one that interested her

When I had about given up on trying to interest her, she decided to turn the conversation in her direction. Making a nimble and graceful leap from her high perch to the floor, with her tail straight in the air, she took several steps in my direction and addressed me on the subject of dinner—her dinner. She gave me a very audible meow and sat with her tail tapping the rug.

She found fault with my message

I tried pleading with her, asking if dinner couldn't wait a minute while we talked. Putting her paw down firmly on such disinteresting talk, she stood, arched her tail, and narrowed her eyes. Then, gathering her feet, she jumped to the couch. Her meow was now one of acute impatience.

She played down my feelings and stressed her own

"Don't you care that I'm sad?" I asked. While I spoke to her she kneaded the couch, hooking her claws in and out of its covering. She began

a fake purr of contentment, which vibrated from
her closed mouth. This purr was a ploy, a scrap
of fake friendliness she was throwing me in an
effort to con me into moving toward the kitchen
and opening a can of cat food. The claws working
in and out of the couch cover gave away her real
feelings of impatience.

She spoke out in anger

Finally, with her whiskers sticking out like radar
antenna, she stood and leaped from the couch.
Full of pride she stalked toward the kitchen, then
paused near the doorway. Her tail switched, and
in a burst of short meows she told me what she
thought of me.

Some Siblings Listen Just Like This Cat

If Ginger, an animal, can seem rude and indifferent
when someone appeals to her, how much worse it
becomes when brothers and sisters treat one another
in a similar manner.

 Some siblings communicate just like this cat, ig-
noring pleas, interrupting with their own needs, finding fault, or changing the subject to one in which they
are interested. Do you communicate like this cat?

The Case of the Amiable Dog

In the example that follows a dog takes the part of
the good communicator. Are your communication
manners as good as this dog's?

He used good body language

We moved along at an easy lope, our legs seemed
in unison, our spirits high. Billy was the kind of

dog that would run until he dropped if I wanted to run. His unfailing devotion didn't end at running either. His good manners and amiable disposition extended to close communication. He listened while I talked and showed an interest in what I was saying.

At the end of the jogging trail we dropped to the grass. I was puffing. Billy panted. "It's a good day for a run isn't it old boy?" I stroked Billy's silky head. He thumped his tail and put his muzzle in my lap.

He responded to my mood

Lying back in the grass, I looked up at the evening sky and watched a cloud drift by overhead. Billy lay perfectly still waiting for my next words. He was content that nothing at all need be said between us.

He didn't try to finish my sentences

"I've got an idea." I spoke to Billy and yet I was speaking to myself. "What do you say about going . . ." I broke off midsentence, letting the question dangle as I mentally changed my mind. Billy didn't stir. He didn't whine or nudge me, demanding to know what I had been about to say. He waited patiently for my next words.

He didn't interrupt with demands

Quietly, we continued to lie in the grass. Then I heard Billy's stomach growl, and unconsciously he licked his lips. I looked at my watch. It was time to get moving. The light was fading. It was past Billy's supper time, not that he'd ever remind me. Good-natured and patient, even when hungry, he continued to lie in the grass, his large, limpid eyes watching me, waiting to see what I wanted to do next.

He didn't try to hurry a subject along

"Time to head home," I said to Billy. He yelped happily and stood waiting and wagging his tail until I gave the signal to start. Deliberately, I paused, testing his patience. Without a whine or a fidget he sat back on his haunches. I smiled and slapped my side; we started off on a run. The harmony of our movement was again one as we trotted home, companions and friends.

Few Siblings Have the Communication Manners of a Dog

Do you sit and listen quietly while your sibling is speaking? Do you resist picking a piece of lint from your coat or looking around the room to see what else is going on when what your sibling has to say doesn't interest you? Do you stare blankly at the ceiling or over your sibling's head instead of nodding and indicating that you are listening?

Responding to a sibling's changing emotions seems to be something brothers and sisters often do rather poorly. If your sibling tries to be funny and you aren't in the mood for laughter, do you begrudge your sibling even a smile? If your sibling wants to be serious, do you fail to pick up on this mood? Do you react to certain words and tune out anything else your sibling says? Do you criticize or judge your sibling, give unasked-for advice, interpret motives, or make fun of your brother's or sister's opinions? How many dogs have you seen act this way?

Too bad we can't copy a few communication manners from dogs.

What Kind of Communicator Are You?

Ask yourself these communication questions to rate your listening and response skills. Answer either "Yes" or "No" to each question.

When your sibling is speaking do you:

1. Concentrate on what your sibling is saying and shut out other distractions?

   Yes _____   No _____

2. Guard against reacting to emotional words?

   Yes _____   No _____

3. Take care not to interrupt?

   Yes _____   No _____

4. Allow your sibling to finish sentences without jumping to conclusions?

   Yes _____   No _____

5. Take care not to find fault with what your sibling is saying?

   Yes _____   No _____

6. Look at your sibling?

   Yes _____   No _____

When you speak to your sibling do you:

1. Speak about what interests your sibling?

Yes _____   No _____

2. Try not to let your mood dominate the conversation?

Yes _____   No _____

3. Look at your sibling?

Yes _____   No _____

4. Speak slowly and distinctly, expressing your thoughts clearly?

Yes _____   No _____

5. Give your sibling a chance to reply before you go on to your next thought?

Yes _____   No _____

Analysis: These questions are designed to show you where you are supporting good communication habits and where you are failing to let your sibling come really close because you have poor listening and speaking skills. For every "No" response you gave to a question, try to work hard to correct your communication skills in that area.

Plans to enjoy new closeness with your sibling will have a poor chance of succeeding without good communication. Don't be satisfied with your ability as a communicator until you can pass this test with a 100 percent "Yes" score.

Remember, listening is more than just not talking, and talking is more than just expressing your own thoughts. If you need a reason to improve your communication skills, let that reason be your desire for renewed sibling closeness.

Chapter 11 in a Nutshell

Failure to listen is the major cause of poor communication. Good communicators practice these learned skills.

- They listen to what is being said and do not allow themselves to become distracted.
- They take their mood and subject cues from the person who is speaking.
- They are nonjudgmental.
- They do not interrupt.
- They keep on a subject until it is finished.
- They look at the speaker and indicate they are listening.
- They remember what they hear and give thoughtful replies.

12

Learn to Solve Problems

This chapter reviews some perplexing and difficult problems that can divide siblings and keep them apart. The discussion is not meant to discourage you, but rather to offer suggestions on some of the ways to lighten the impact of these difficulties or, better still, show you how to avoid such situations altogether.

Any problem has the potential of becoming serious if ignored. While some situations elude complete solution, an attempt at solving a difficulty may go a long way toward rendering it less harmful. For this purpose, four different categories of adult-sibling relationship problems are defined, and probable solutions to these problems are discussed. The four categories are:

1. problems created by your sibling,
2. problems brought on by others,
3. you as the problem,
4. problems relating to the times.

Perhaps being aware of these areas will enable you to prevent some problems before they start.

Problems Created by Your Sibling

Even in the most amiable sibling relationships problems caused by attitudes or habits may surface from time to time. At the first indication of such a problem brewing, every effort should be made to find a quick solution. The earlier a solution is sought, the sooner good relations can resume. Sometimes simple and direct attempts to solve problems can clear up these situations rather easily, as the following examples illustrate.

Sibling-generated Problems	*Your Solution*
Your sibling wants to borrow money.	Explain that borrowing can lead to resentment on both sides. If you have the means, make your sibling a gift of the asked-for cash.
Your sibling has an addiction.	Don't judge or condemn your sibling. Offer to get him or her professional help.
Your sibling makes too many unreasonable demands on your time.	Explain that you will set aside time that is for the two of you exclusively and hold to a schedule unless there is an emergency.
Your sibling is constantly finding fault with you and your family.	One way of quieting a critic is to admit that you aren't perfect and own up to mistakes and weaknesses before your sibling mentions them.
Your sibling expects you to make all the reaching-out gestures. The phone bill is always yours.	This is where communication comes in. Ask your sibling to answer your letters and to take turns calling you.

Problems Created by Outsiders

Siblings need to learn to deal with the many distractions and problems from outside sources. Such problems can come between siblings and destroy their relationship. Outsiders—a spouse, an employer, another sibling, a parent, a friend—can become a threat to sibling closeness when they cause problems. The following suggestions will help you cope with some of the "outsider problems" you may encounter as adult siblings.

Problems Created by Outsiders	*Your Solution*
Your spouse doesn't like your sibling.	Keep your sibling and your contentious spouse apart. Make the time to see your sibling privately.
Your best friend is jealous of your sibling.	See your sibling without your friend. Brothers and sisters were part of your life before friends.
Your employer equates your reputation with your sibling's problems.	Work to be accepted on your own merit, and communicate this effort to your employer.
One of your siblings is jealous of the brother or sister to whom you are showing the most attention.	Include the jealous sibling in a group outing and then single him or her out for a little extra attention.
Your mother pits you and your sibling against each other to drive a wedge between you and gain more attention for herself.	Discuss the matter with your sibling and form a united front to ignore your mother's devisive attempts.

You as the Problem

Sibling reconciliation calls for an investment of your personal time and a moral obligation to continue with a renewed relationship once you have encouraged closeness. You cannot shower a sibling with attention one month and walk away the next. Once you enter a new phase of a relationship, it is irresponsible and unkind to go back to a past, uncaring time.

Even a caring sibling can do things to destroy a valued relationship, but solutions to these problems are in your own pocket as the following suggestions will show you.

You as the Problem	*Your Solution*
You become easily discouraged when your sibling doesn't respond to your overtures to establish renewed contact.	Keep busy with new contact ideas and don't try to tally up unsuccessful attempts.
You are stumped by unknowns that crop up and prevent you from carrying out your plans.	Be flexible enough to revise your plans.
You get lazy and set aside plans to contact your sibling.	Talk to your friends who have close siblings and get exposed to their energy and enthusiasm.
You run into personal problems such as illness, debts, or family difficulties.	Ask for help. Maybe your sibling would welcome the chance to be needed.
You keep slipping back into old habits that annoy your sibling.	Say you are trying to change. Enlist your sibling's help in making that change.

Problems Relating to the Times

Job pressures, high rents, long commutes, aging parents who need your attention, and even your own demands on yourself are just a few of the problems inherent in the times. But many of these problems of the nineties have remedies, as the following suggestions indicate.

Problems of the Nineties	*Your Solution*
You live a long distance from your siblings.	Scattered families need to learn to write letters frequently, share family snapshots, make telephone calls, and plan vacations together.
Job and family pressures	Tell yourself you will set aside just twenty minutes per week for your sibling. You can write a short note or make a phone call in that much time. Later, try to find longer periods of time for your sibling.
Children of divorce	Half brothers and sisters can be linked with each other by ties as strong as siblings with the same two parents, and don't let anyone tell you otherwise.
Greed	Build closeness on generosity. Never mind trying to get one step up on your sibling. Instead, share good fortune when it comes.

The Two Most Dangerous Times for Sibling Love

Probably the two most frequent examples siblings give when they are asked to mention what caused difficulties between them are:

1. the division of their parents' estate,
2. planning too much togetherness.

These two dangerous situations can be managed with sensible and cooperative action on the part of all siblings involved. Just being forewarned that these two problems exist can go a long way toward preventing bad feelings.

Here follow some practical suggestions that have helped other sibling relationships survive these situations intact.

Surviving an Estate Division

One of the most divisive times in the lives of siblings is when their parents die and it is time to divide up the property left in the family estate. Jealousy over who gets mother's best china or dad's golf clubs can divide brothers and sisters for life. The best way to prevent this kind of bitterness is to set up a plan for each sibling in turn to choose a piece of property, drawing lots for the sibling who gets first choice. Continue to make rounds of choices until all the small property has been divided. Divide funds and major pieces of property according to your parents' will, and don't hold it against your siblings if one or the other were willed more than you were. Remember, the will was of your parents' making.

A little unselfish giving on your part may help a tug-of-war over property. Offer your sibling the best piece of furniture or an admired etching. Sometimes generosity can be contagious. If you make a generous and unsolicited offer, your sibling may return one.

The best thing to remember in the heat of estate division is to tell yourself that no material thing, not a rug, not a vase, not a pair of high-powered binoculars are worth near as much as your sibling's love.

Avoiding Too Much Togetherness

Being close to your sibling is desirable when you both have the freedom to move in an out of the relationship and continue with your own private adult lives. Too much closeness can lead to stress and promote conflict. When you and your sibling know too much about each other's lives, it can be hard for you not to give unasked for advice. Small human imperfections and innocent vices can loom large and reprehensible when you are thrown into too frequent contact. If you are inclined to be even slightly impatient with your sibling, then too much togetherness can become even more dangerous.

To avoid feelings of being smothered on either side, guard against situations that foster too much closeness. The following examples point out joint ventures to watch out for.

- *Shared family vacations*—One mountain cabin and too many family members can be worse than mosquitoes.
- *Partnerships*—Even business success can bring on reinvestment squabbles. Failures can lead to accusations and fault finding.
- *Property that is jointly owned*—Don't share the ownership of things like fishing boats, vacation homes, or a riding horse with your sibling. One sibling may get more use out of the property than the other. This can lead to jealousy.
- *Creative collaboration*—Siblings who do things like writing a book together, building a house

together, or planting a community garden together can get into a row when it is time to
divide the spoils.

Talk it over with your sibling and determine just
how much closeness you can both tolerate. Cut togetherness short of the exasperation point.

Chapter 12 in a Nutshell

- Problems created by your sibling can be solved
  or avoided by showing compassion and using
  communication.
- Problems created by outsiders can be lessened
  when you set aside time to see your sibling alone.
- Problems created by you can be solved by re-
  thinking your plans and changing your attitude.
- Problems of the nineties call for a dedication
  to renewal based on a willingness to share some
  of your already crowded days.
- Circumvent the two most dangerous causes for
  sibling separation.

  1. When dividing your parents' estate, be fair
     about sharing.
  2. Avoid too much togetherness.

13

Add Up Your
Gains and Losses

This chapter offers three suggestions that may help you in your plan to build a closer relationship with your sibling.

1. The first is that you evaluate the progress of your plans on a regular basis. A short checklist is supplied to help you with this evaluation.

2. The second is that you inventory the hidden gains you may enjoy as a bonus to sibling closeness.

3. And last is a word of caution to prepare you for the possibility that your renewal efforts could come to less than you had hoped for.

A Quick Checklist to See How You Are Doing

Once you have started on your relationship renewal campaign you should try to take stock at least monthly to see how your plan is progressing. This evaluation process does not need to be complicated or time-consuming. Just check your efforts against the following questions and decide whether you rate a "Yes" or a "No" answer.

1. Did I phone my sibling at least once this month?

Yes _____   No _____

2. Have I been writing to my sibling on a regular basis?

Yes _____   No _____

3. Did I visit my sibling when I said I would?

Yes _____   No _____

4. Do I know more about my sibling in the following categories than I did one month ago?

- health, physical   Yes _____   No _____
- health, mental   Yes _____   No _____
- needs (if any)   Yes _____   No _____
- problems (if any)   Yes _____   No _____

If your "Yes" answers far outweigh your "No" answers, you are doing a good job of meeting your goals. Your next step might be to:

- Set your goals up another notch.
- If you have more than one sibling you may want to begin a relationship renewal campaign with a second member of your family.

Too many "No" answers can mean you need to look at your plans again and strengthen your approach where you have fallen short of your goals.

- Maybe you started out well enough on your plan to be a better sibling but now your efforts have dropped off.
- Maybe you came swooping down on your sibling with such fanfare that your brother or sister backed off.

- Maybe you have worked very hard to come closer to your sibling but have seen no spark of interest from the other side.

The Hidden Gains of Sibling Closeness

Try not to be too discouraged if at first your attempts to come closer to your sibling are not accepted immediately. Success may be just another phone call away. In case you need a little encouragement to keep up your spirits, the stories that follow will give you some idea of a few of the additional rewards, besides the obvious one of sibling closeness, that renewed sibling contact can bring.

I know myself better

I find that in getting to know my older brother after all these years I'm discovering a few things about myself that I wasn't aware of before. My brother has begun to tell me some of the things he remembers about our parents when they were young, and about me when I was a baby. Since our parents are now dead, this glimpse of my personal history could never have been given by any person other than my only sibling.

My other friendships are improving

Since I've become aware of the need to reach out to my sibling on a regular basis I'm trying to become a more helpful and considerate friend as well. I call or write to my friends more often. I ask my friends if I can help them. I'm trying to be a better all-around person to both my siblings and my friends. All of my relationships seem to be going better.

I think I'm a better parent

Since getting back together with my brother and spending some time talking about our childhood I've been thinking about my children more. I am trying to give my son and daughter a chance to be close to each other as young siblings. I helped my daughter bake cookies to surprise her brother. My brother reminded me that I used to bake for him. I taught my son that he should watch out for his little sister when they crossed streets on the way to school. I remember now that my brother used to watch out for me.

I understand my husband's family better

I have only one sister, but my husband comes from a large and loving family. Getting closer to my sister has helped me see my husband's family in a new light. I'm learning to copy some of their family ways and offer my sister the kind of love my husband's siblings show to one another. I also have a better understanding of my husband's need to be with his siblings.

I feel less stressed

I thought that adding the additional responsibility of making contact with my sister would only add to the rush and stress of my already overcrowded schedule. Strange, but just the opposite has happened. I've learned to budget time for my sister and manage the rest of my time better, too.

I'm less worried about the care of our aging parents

For some reason I took it on myself to decide that I would be the only one interested in making the decisions and taking over all the care of our parents when they could no longer help themselves. Since growing closer to my sister I realize that she has full intention of sharing this responsibility. I just never asked her before.

I got rid of an old grudge

It was perfectly silly for a grown woman to go around holding a grudge about something that happened two decades ago, but that is just what I was doing. When we were in high school my younger sister charmed a boyfriend of mine right out from under my nose. I'd been counting on his invitation to the Christmas dance and he asked her instead. Until last month when we got to talking about that date I hadn't forgiven her. When she told me about what a rotten time she'd had that evening, the first thing I knew we were laughing together about it. Feels good not to have that chip on my shoulder anymore.

My brother helped me break a bad habit

For years I've been wanting to quit smoking but I could never get motivated to do so. My brother told me that he quit and he knew I could do it, too. He kept encouraging me and supporting my effort, and the first thing I knew I was free of cigarettes. I haven't smoked in four months thanks to my brother's help.

Sometimes There Are Losses

It wouldn't be honest or realistic to say that all renewal plans go smoothly and end in happy relationships. Sometimes efforts are ignored, doors are slammed, and discouragement is the end product of your plans and efforts to come closer to your sibling. There are two possible realities you may have to face when you go into any new or renewed relationship with a sibling, especially if you haven't been in contact with that brother or sister for a long time.

1. Some siblings no longer want to be close.

2. Some siblings have changed so much and have grown so far away from the past they feel they have no basis for relationship renewal.

The stories that follow illustrate dead-end relationships, but if you are the kind of person who never gives up you may be able to breathe life into any type of situation.

When is it time to admit defeat

I went to my brother with high hopes for renewed closeness. I was willing to expend all the effort, happy to try over and over again to surmount any resistance he might have to getting back together. I failed to win him over. He just wasn't interested in me.

If this happens you have to ask yourself whether it is time to give up on the idea of sibling closeness. Again, this is where communication can help. If all your attempts at reconciliation have failed, if your letters go unanswered, if your sibling doesn't want to talk to you on the phone or see you in person, it is time to ask your sibling why closeness is a problem. If your sibling is holding a grudge, see if you can make things right. Be willing to try to change things. But if the bottom line reads "uninterested," you may have to accept the fact that sometimes "No" means "No" and it is time for you to back off for a while. Mark your calendar and try contacting your sibling again in a few months, but be prepared for a long uphill climb.

My sibling had changed

My brother is no longer anything like the person he was as a kid. We lived on a farm when we were young, and we were dirt poor. I was happy there, but my brother always wanted to get off the farm. He's climbed to the top of a corporate success ladder now and he doesn't want to look back. I'm part of the life he wants to forget. I tried keeping in touch but he simply wasn't interested.

Finding that your sibling rejects your overtures can be a sad experience, especially if this is your only sibling. You can wait awhile and give reconciliation another try, but sometimes you have to bend to your sibling's wishes to be left alone.

Chapter 13 in a Nutshell

To keep meeting your goals and advancing your plans you should evaluate your progress at least monthly.

Your renewal of sibling closeness may lead to these additional gains.

- You may get to know yourself better.
- You might find that your other relationships are improving.
- You could become a better parent.
- You may be able to understand your spouse's family better.
- You might find yourself feeling less stressed.

- You may be able to share your worries about aging parents.
- You could get rid of old grudges.
- A sibling may help you break a bad habit.

An attempt at sibling closeness could end in failure if your sibling is really not interested in relationship renewal. You can try again at a later time, but sometimes you have to recognize that "No" really means "No."

14

Guidelines for Ongoing Success

Renewed relationships with your grown siblings are not guaranteed to go on and on in harmony unless you guard against drifting apart again. Good ongoing relationships call for ongoing effort on both sides.

This chapter offers a few suggestions to help make it easy for you to stay in touch.

How to Keep in Contact

Here are some positive suggestions for ongoing relationships. These ideas were offered by siblings who have kept together in loving harmony through many years.

Maybe some of these workable ideas will help you remain in close contact with your siblings.

We give each other a reminder calendar

Every year my sister and I give one another a new calendar on January first. Instead of a blank calendar, we mark the monthly pages with important dates before we give them to each other. I usually write down a day in February when I want my sister to come and visit. And of course, we mark each other's birthdays. My sister makes a vacation suggestion for July on the calendar she gives me. Our exchange calendars keep us from getting too busy and leaving no time for each other.

We plan special time for each other

When we get together for the family dinner at Thanksgiving, my brother and I plan three fishing trips for the coming year. We set the dates and promise each other nothing will come along to get in the way of those fishing trips. By planning ahead we can be sure our lives won't get so busy that we miss out on these times together.

We complete a project together

On my brother's birthday in June we think up a joint project for our summer vacation. One year we made a special photo album of our mountain trip. One year we had a beard-growing contest. Just doing these summer things together helps us to keep close to one another in our thoughts for the rest of the year.

We make one wish come true for each other

Every year for as long as I can remember, my brother and I have told each other a personal wish we would like to see come true. We tell our wish to each other. We keep it fair. We don't ask for impossible or expensive things. Our wishes are small and simple and easy to grant. One year I wished for a red rose bush for my back garden and the next week I awoke one morning to find that my brother had crept into my backyard and planted my wished-for rose during the night. I think about him out there digging in the dark every time I pick a blossom. It was a wonderful way for him to say he loves me.

We make each other one handmade gift each year

My youngest brother and I decided that we would give each other something we had made ourselves each year. Last year my brother made me a wooden garden bench, and whenever I get tired when I am out in the garden I sit on that bench. Of course, while I'm sitting there I think of him. This year I'm knitting my brother a pair of ski sox. We don't wait for special occasions like birthdays or Christmas to exchange our handmade gifts. We give them when they are finished. Just giving a gift for no reason makes that gift all the more special. And when your sibling takes the time to make a gift, that is the best giving of all.

Giving Yourself

Giving doesn't have to mean exchanging gifts. When you take the time to help your sibling in other ways you are giving of yourself by making a gift of your time.

If You Live Near Your Sibling

When you live near your sibling it is possible to hand deliver something you make or to go to your sibling's home and help out in some needed area. After you read the ideas that follow you will probably be able to think of some suggestions that fit your unique situation.

- Bake your sibling's favorite cake and deliver it in time for dinner.

- Mow your sibling's lawn while the family is on vacation.
- Wash your sibling's car.
- Take your sibling's clothes to the Laundromat and then mend any clothes that need attention.
- Offer to do errands one day a month.
- Take your sibling's overdue books back to the library and pay any outstanding fines.
- Take your niece or nephew to a baseball game.
- Wash your sibling's windows, inside and out.
- Take your sibling's dog for a walk.
- Fix something that is broken around your sibling's house.

If You Live at a Distance From Your Sibling

When you live far away from your sibling you can still mail things you make or hire services for your sibling.

Here are just a few long-distance ideas for helping out your sibling.

- Mail some home-baked cookies.
- Find the family's old scratched-out address list and copy a new one for your sibling.
- Self-address and stamp a set of envelopes to make it easier to write to you.
- For a busy sibling, order and pay for some kind of service such as cleaning, gardening, or shopping.

By doing that little something extra, by giving of yourself, you are telling your sibling you care. As long as you keep on caring your relationship cannot slip away.

Guidelines for Continued Closeness

Here is a brief list of guidelines that can help the continuance of any relationship. Other siblings have tried these suggestions and found them helpful and workable. Both you and your sibling should read them and take them to heart.

1. *Solve any problems that come between you as soon as you discover them.* Don't hold your tongue and allow a problem to fester. Communication can be a preventative medicine as well as a cure. If you see a problem looming, sit down with your sibling and talk it out.

2. *Learn to profit by your mistakes;* don't repeat them. Keep away from touchy subjects you know will cause disputes. If you and your sibling argue about politics or religion, talk about food, travel, or some other neutral subject instead. If you don't like your sibling's children, arrange meetings free of families.

3. *When you make a mistake say, "I'm sorry," and mean it.* Never offer excuses instead of apologies. Tell your sibling you will try to remember not to repeat your error.

4. *When your sibling makes a mistake never rub it in* or say, "I told you so." When you're right keep quiet and don't gloat.

5. *Don't turn your relationship into a power struggle.* Trying to get one up on your sibling can turn harmony into a contentious situation that leaves little room for closeness.

6. *Don't go back to taking your sibling for granted.* When you stop calling, writing, and visiting your brother or sister the renewed closeness that you have so carefully cultivated can soon slip away.

Chapter 14 in a Nutshell

- Set goals to keep together and help one another to meet those goals.
- Give of yourself, your time, and your talents in small ways to show your love.
- An ongoing harmonious relationship with your sibling calls for an ongoing effort on both sides.

15

A Sibling Code of Ethics

In this chapter we are going to talk about siblings and ethics and the importance of dealing fairly with your siblings even when your choices are difficult.

What Are Ethics?

Ethics are those inherent guidelines that keep you from losing your sense of direction in today's busy and sometimes indifferent world. Ethics are those invisible precepts that can help you make the vital and sometimes tough decisions you may face on a day-to-day basis. Ethics help you to be a better sibling and to come out feeling good about yourself.

Your Sibling Code of Ethics

The code that follows is straightforward and practical because today's world is fraught with decision hazards that are complicated enough. Based on a keen sense of right and wrong, this simple compendium is designed to help you make choices, act upon your decisions, stand by your convictions, and do a better job of being a better sibling.

Before you begin to study this code, however, a

word about its application is wise. It has been said that ethics are the rules that help you decide right from wrong. But please remember that no set of rules can account for all situations. There is little in the world of human interaction that is all black or white. Fairness often lies in the gray area in between. Ethics can mean acting on something or having the courage to wait out a situation. Ethics can be speaking up or holding your tongue. Sometimes ethics require that you take a difficult stand when there is no guarantee that your decision will be right. When you make a bad call, the best you can do is to try to mend the wrong you have done and learn by your mistakes. A willingness to learn, to start over, is part of being ethical.

Each of the eight sections of the code that follows includes a case history of a sibling who coped with a problem involving a stated ethical standard. Some of the decisions were less than perfect because the people involved were, after all, human.

1. Give Your Best Effort

There will be times when you are tired or busy, when it will be easier not to help your sibling, not to visit, not to write, not to be enthusiastic about some plan your sibling promotes—but you should strive to give your best to every contact with your sibling. Some ideas will challenge your imagination. Other sibling projects will seem tedious and boring. To make up for your disinterest in some of your sibling's suggestions, put a little more of yourself into these plans. Plans have a way of developing into something interesting when you give them your best. The following story illustrates just such a turnaround.

The trip to icky sticky state park

My brother has always been an outdoor man. As a kid he would have slept out in the backyard, even in the snow, if our parents had allowed him to. Even today, in middle age, he climbs mountains, shoots rapids, camps in the wilderness, and calls all of this good fun. I'm just the opposite. My idea of an outing includes a nice clean motel room with a heated swimming pool three steps from the door. When my brother invited me for a weekend camp-out at his favorite state park, I put up all kinds of excuses not to go. I said I didn't have a sleeping bag. He dug up an extra one to loan me. I said I was out of shape and couldn't hike very far. He offered to stay near the campground. Finally, I gave in and off we went. I was afraid of being bitten by ticks, attacked by bears, swarmed by mosquitoes, and catching my death of cold. I worried and complained all the way to the park. My brother was quiet. Finally, I began to be ashamed of myself. I thought about how my brother had taken such care to plan the outing. For his sake I decided to put on a happy face. When we got to the campground I threw myself into unpacking and setting up. To my surprise I began to have fun. My brother and I began to laugh together and talk about things we hadn't discussed in years. That trip taught me how important it is to give your best to your sibling even when you are asked to do something that you don't think you'll like.

2. *Pace Yourself*

Learn how much time you can set aside for your sibling. Determine how many hours you can take out of each week or each month to give your sibling and save that time for your sibling alone. Don't start out by smothering your sibling with attention and then find you do not have the time to keep up the pace. Being a "sibling starter"—a person who promises everything but fails to finish much of anything—can damage your relationship beyond repair. Learn to commit yourself only to the amount of time you can comfortably spare on an ongoing basis. Make only those promises you know you can keep. The following story illustrates the folly of making lavish promises you can't keep.

Here-today-and-gone-tomorrow Tommy

I was going to be such a good brother. Every week I was going to take my newly widowed sister to lunch, offer to help her with her shopping, do the repairs around her house, even take on paying some of her bills. When I started to pile on promises, my sister showed me that she was smarter than I was. She knew I had a demanding job, a big family, and maybe even less money than she had. She steered me away from making promises I couldn't keep.

3. Admit Your Mistakes

Because you are human, and not a machine, your plans for getting back together with your grown siblings may be fraught with false starts and even dumb mistakes. No matter how hard you work to avoid these mistakes, sooner or later your sibling relationship is going to run up against a problem. Don't kick sand over your problem. Bring it out into the open and talk it out with your sibling. If you have been wrong, admit your mistake and begin at once to decide what you can do to make amends. The following story about name-calling illustrates a common mistake.

Bigfoot is not a loving name

I called my brother-in-law "Bigfoot" and it nearly cost me my sister's love. Sure he has big feet, but so do I. I have a sharp, unkind tongue, too. Call me "Big Mouth" and you would be correct. How could I have been so stupid? Calling names when I was trying to reach out and win back my sister's love was the worst possible mistake. I said I was sorry and admitted I was wrong. At least we're speaking now, but I know it will take a long time for my sister and her husband to forget my thoughtlessness.

4. Stand by Your Convictions

Maybe your sibling needs you to take a stand on a debatable question. Before you agree, study the subject from all sides and weigh the consequences of your support. Make judgments based on what you know, not on what you are told. Make your decisions based on knowledge and backed by what you feel is right. It is much better to tell your sibling right off if you can't back a position than to say "Yes" and flip over to "No." Once you have made your decision, unless factors change, stand by that decision. You may need courage to disagree in the face of pressure, but fairness calls for consistency. The following story illustrates how difficult it can be to make fair decisions.

A house divided

When our mother died my older brother John and his family wanted to move into the family home. The estate had been left to all three of us brothers. John said he'd pay my younger brother, Frank, and me rent and keep up the house, and we could always sell it later. Frank wanted to sell the house at once. He said he needed a lump sum of cash not just a little rent money. I wasn't in urgent need of the cash so I could have let the house go either way. However, because I thought selling the house and dividing the cash was what my parents had intended I sided with my younger brother and the house was sold. It was not an easy decision, but my older brother said he appreciated the fact I had based that decision on what I thought was fair.

5. Keep Secrets

When your sibling tells you something in confidence, keep this information to yourself. If you tell just one person you have no guarantee that person won't tell another. Guard your sibling's secrets as if they were your own. The following story of carelessness shows how easy it is to betray a trust.

The forgotten letter

My brother wrote to tell me his marriage was in trouble. His wife wanted a divorce because of his drinking. He asked for my help. He'd run up some debts, and his creditors were making his life even more miserable. Unthinking, I left my brother's letter lying on the kitchen table when I went off to work. My nosy cousin, who was visiting for a few days, picked it up and read it. Now the whole family knows about my brother's problem. I betrayed a trust with carelessness.

6. Earn Your Own Way

If you want a better relationship with your sibling, expect that the effort to renew closeness will be yours. Don't ask your spouse, your aging parents, or even your own children to do the spade work for you. Reconciliation won at the expense of others will not bring you any real closeness. Earn your sibling's love one day at a time, yourself. The following story of a man too busy to let his sister know he cared for her illustrates how lonely that position can be.

Seeing less of Sally

I expected my wife to take the time to bring my sister and me back together. I wanted the benefits but none of the work of closeness. I hadn't been much of a brother for years and all of a sudden I decided I'd really like to see more of Sally. I asked my wife to cook a fancy dinner and ask Sally over. At the last minute I had a business meeting and didn't even get home until Sally had left. My wife said she enjoyed the evening. I felt left out. I asked my wife to get tickets for the three of us to go to the symphony, but I went to an out-of-town conference that weekend and the seat next to my sister stayed empty. I'm no closer to my sister now than I was two months ago, but my wife and Sally are getting along fine. I've promised myself I'll earn my own way to renewed closeness with Sally.

7. *Abide by the Rules*

Good relationships thrive on the rules of fair exchange. Being fair means maintaining a balance. When you and your sibling get back together, don't try to be the whole show. Togetherness calls for two-way communication. Let your renewed relationship be one with a balance of give-and-take between you. If you need to be needed, remember that your siblings do, too. If you and your sibling agree to give a certain amount of time to each other, honor one another's birthdays with gifts, and share family tasks, then abide by those agreements and keep them to the letter of the law. Your renewed relationship will be only as good as your word. The following story of a sibling who thought love was a power struggle illustrates the futility of this position.

Jumping the gun

To my brother a loving relationship is a little like a foot race. He always has to be out in front. When we agree to share the check at lunch he makes a show of grabbing it and paying. When we decide between us to give simple, inexpensive gifts for Christmas he buys me expensive jewelry. I've asked him to keep to our agreement and he just laughs. I'm not laughing.

8. Avoid Judgments

Remind yourself that making an unkind judgment is the quickest way to kill your sibling's love. Ask yourself before you speak whether what you are about to say is something you would want to hear about yourself. Finding fault can eat holes in the fabric of closeness. Don't judge your sibling like the sister in the story that follows.

Accept me for who I am

I can not remember a time when my sister wasn't judging me. According to her I went to the wrong school, took the wrong job, and married the wrong man. I love my sister but I want her to accept me and my choices for what they are—*my* choices.

The Hidden Rewards of Good Ethics

Good ethics have the obvious reward of giving you the feeling that you are doing the right thing, but there are a couple hidden rewards you may enjoy when you live by the sibling code just spelled out.

- Good ethics have a way of being contagious. When you treat your sibling fairly, you are more

likely to receive fair treatment in return.
- Good ethics allow you to be at peace with yourself.

The Essence

In a final analysis, the real and basic nature of the sibling code of ethics can be summed up in two statements.

- *Be there* when your sibling needs you.
- *Be fair* to your sibling.

This code isn't new. It is as old as the need to make choices.

Chapter 15 in a Nutshell

This code of ethics will help you deal fairly with your sibling.

- Make only those promises you can keep.
- Admit your mistakes and do what you can to make amends.
- To be fair, be consistent.
- Keep your sibling's secrets confidential.
- Earn your sibling's love yourself.
- Abide by the agreements the two of you decide upon.
- Don't judge your sibling.

Good ethics can be contagious, and they allow you to be at peace with yourself.

16

The ABC's of Sibling Relationships

This chapter contains a minidictionary of the practical sibling-relationship suggestions that have appeared throughout this book. Here are several ways you can use these suggestions to help renew and improve your relationships with your siblings.

- Mark the ideas that especially apply to your situation and share them with your sibling.
- Use an individual idea as a heading on your next letter to your sibling.
- Copy a definition and post it on your refrigerator to remind yourself to practice what it says.
- Adopt a monthly quote and write it on a bookmark where you will see it each time you pick up your current reading.
- Use the vocabulary as a review tool to refresh your memory about the many helpful suggestions that appear throughout the book.

The more often you use these ABC's, the more you will realize how basic they are to building a good relationship with your sibling.

Here they are from A to Z. Put them to use.

Accept. Good siblings accept their brothers and sisters for what they are, not what can be made of them.

Action. When your planning is finished, don't put off the action stage of sibling relationship renewal.

Alienate. For lack of thought, many of us continue to do the things we know will alienate our siblings.

Amends. When you make a mistake, say you are sorry and try to make amends.

Ask. Ask your sibling questions and show an interest in the answers.

Assessment. Assessment of your present relationship with your sibling can help you break the mold of failure.

Assumption. Never assume you know all about your sibling. Ask your sibling to tell you things; don't fill in the blanks yourself.

Attitude. Your desire to be helpful and to get to know your sibling better will go a long way toward making a renewed relationship possible.

Awareness. To begin to renew a positive relationship with your sibling you must first be aware of the weaknesses and strengths of your early life experiences to avoid old mistakes and build on what was good.

Bad tempered. Remain calm and courteous in the face of sibling indifference and tactlessness.

Basics. It is basic to find out about your sibling's needs and wants before you try to fill them.

Belabor. Never belabor a point you are trying to make. This comes across as bossy and dictatorial.

Believe. Show that you believe in your sibling and he or she will be more willing to accept you.

Body language. Let your gestures, your expressions, your smiles, show your sibling how you are feeling.

Bonus. Sibling love can be one of life's bonuses.

Brag. Don't brag about what you have and make comparisons to your sibling's lot.

Calendar. Keep a marked calendar of dates with your sibling, both past and upcoming, to remind yourself to keep in contact year-round.

Caring. A good basic adjective for any good sibling relationship is the word caring.

Change. Believe change is possible.

Cheerful. Nothing creates a loving impression faster than a smile and a cheerful greeting.

Communication. Two-way communication is basic to sibling trust and love. Problems have a way of dissolving when they are talked out.

Competition. A sibling relationship should not become a power struggle or a foot race. Mutually agree on the rules of your relationship and stick to the rules.

Complaints. Listen to what your sibling is saying and try to respond promptly if you are the cause of a problem.

Confidential. Keep what your sibling tells you secret.

Convictions. Make decisions based on what you know is right and stand by your convictions.

Courtesy. Sibling love thrives on small gestures of courtesy like a helping hand or words of appreciation.

Credibility. Do not make promises you cannot fulfill or you will ruin your credibility rating.

Criticize. Siblings who criticize put distance between themselves and brothers and sisters they love.

Cry. Don't cry on your sibling's shoulder. Bring your good news and your joys to your siblings.

Dependable. A worthy sibling is dependable and worthy of trust.

Diligence. A good relationship depends upon a diligent and earnest effort to keep up with ongoing goals.

Distance. Miles need not stand between you and a good sibling relationship.

Easy. When winning and holding your sibling's love begins to look too easy, the time has come to guard against arrogance.

Echo. Conversation with your sibling should never be a repetition of echoed, patronizing phrases.

Empty. As long as your sibling lives your life never need be empty.

Enthusiasm. Accept your sibling's suggestions and plans with enthusiasm.

Erode. Time and distance can erode your sibling relationship if you do not take care to keep love alive.

Ethics. Good ethics are basic to an honest and fair sibling relationship.

Evaluate. Ongoing evaluations of your relationship status will prevent backsliding on goals.

Excuses. Lame excuses are the dry rot of closeness.

Explain. Trust is built on honesty. Always explain your motives for what you ask your sibling to do.

Fair. To win your sibling's love and respect stay free of bias and offer fair treatment.

Faults. Don't point out your sibling's faults. Try to mention good qualities instead.

First. A sibling relationship is not a foot race. Never try to best your sibling. You don't need to come out first, just fair.

Flexible. Be flexible. Keep plans open for change and be ready to move goals on to higher aspirations.

Focus. Focus your attention on winning one sibling at a time.

Follow-up. Keep renewal plans alive on an ongoing basis. Never make a promise and not follow up.

Forgiving. Forgive yesterday's shortcomings and get on with tomorrow.

Friendships. However close, friendships cannot replace blood ties.

Gains. The gains you make in renewing a sibling relationship will be in direct proportion to the amount of effort you expend.

Gifts. Give your sibling small gifts for no special reason other than to say, "I love you."

Goals. Set goals pointing toward future kin caring.

Grievances. Settle old grievances, forget past slights, and go on to tomorrow with a clean slate.

Gripes. Listen when your sibling has gripes. This is how you learn to make improvements.

Growing. Plan new activities and shared projects to keep your renewed relationship growing.

Guessing. Second guessing what your sibling is thinking instead of using honest channels of communication isn't fair to you or your sibling.

Guilt trips. Don't lay guilt trips. If your sibling feels compelled to be close to you only out of a feeling of forced obligation, nobody's true emotional needs will be satisfied.

Haste. You cannot rush into a good relationship. Lay out your plans and follow up slowly and with thought.

Health. One of the things you should know about your siblings is the state of their physical and mental health.

Help. Offer your siblings your help before it is necessary for them to ask for it.

Honesty. Give kind, but honest answers when your siblings ask for your opinions.

Hopeful. Recognizing the weaknesses in your sibling relationships can be a hopeful sign. When you know where ties are weak you have a basis for building stronger ones.

Humor. Laugh at yourself and with your siblings—not at them.

Hurdles. Take hurdles one at a time; they do not seem so high that way.

Ideas. Listen to your sibling's new ideas and be willing to accept the need for change.

Illness. When illness isolates your sibling, double your efforts to be helpful.

Impartial. Remain apart from and impartial in your sibling's family disputes.

Important. Give your siblings the feeling that their interests and problems are important to you.

Indifference. The two key reasons siblings drift apart are indifference and the assumption that your sibling will always be there for you.

Individual. Build your relationships with your siblings one sibling at a time.

Influences. Guard your sibling relationships against destructive outside influences.

Insurance. Finding out about what not to do can be good insurance for starting out right.

Interference. Adult siblings have a right to their own privacy without interference from their brothers and sisters.

Interrupt. Don't interrupt your sibling to talk about ideas of your own.

Invite. When you invite your brother or sister on an outing make it easy to accept. Set a time that is convenient and pick a place that is easy to reach.

January. Don't wait until the first of the year to turn over a new leaf. You can begin sibling relationship renewal plans on any day.

Jealousy. Forget old resentments and start anew with your sibling.

Job. A job, however valuable, can never replace a sibling. Don't use work as an excuse not to see your brothers and sisters.

Journal. Keep a log of sibling contacts, write down failures and successes, and build on what you have done right.

Judgments. Avoid judging your sibling. Finding fault is not the path to renewed relationships.

Justify. Never try to justify your mistakes. If you hurt your sibling, apologize and try to make amends.

Key. The key to understanding your sibling's needs is listening.

Kindness. Kindness is often returned with like treatment.

Knowledge. The more you know about your sibling the better your chance of being close.

Lacking. Siblings who are self-centered and uncaring can lack the basic component for good bonding.

Lapse. A lapse in caring can mean a heavy loss in your sibling's belief in your sincerity.

Late. Arriving late for an appointment, or remembering a sibling's birthday after the date, are just two ways of saying your sibling isn't very important to you.

Leeway. Give your siblings plenty of leeway to do what they want. Guard against too much togetherness.

Letters. Little notes sent often are worth more than eight page letters sent infrequently.

Lifestyle. Learn to accept that your sibling's lifestyle might not fit in with your own.

Listen. Listen to what your sibling says first and then try to give answers and fill needs.

Love. Don't be embarrassed to tell your siblings you love them. Say it out loud and write it in your letters.

Loyalty. When you are loyal to your sibling and put that person ahead of friends and strangers, you will find that loyalty will be returned twofold.

Mature. As an adult sibling you should exhibit mature judgment and put aside childish differences.

Memory. Recalling happy times from your childhood can be a powerful bridge to the future.

Money. Don't try to buy sibling love with expensive gifts and lavish entertainment. Money is no substitute for love.

Motivate. Keep setting goals for new plans and shared sibling activities to motivate an ongoing relationship.

Name. Remember what name your sibling prefers to be called and drop baby names left over from childhood that may now be an embarrassment.

Needs. Try to put your sibling's needs ahead of your own and you may find both fulfilled.

Negative. Don't allow negative thoughts to interfere with even slow progress.

Negligence. Failure to attend to small details and promises can lead to the downfall of greater plans.

Objectives. Evaluate your objectives on an ongoing basis and keep up with changing needs.

One. Win back your siblings' love one sibling at a time.

Open-minded. An open mind and a flexible outlook can lend vision to your relationships with your siblings.

Overreact. When in an emotional situation guard against overreacting.

Overwhelm. Tiptoe softly back into your sibling's life. Don't make grand and overwhelming gestures that can seem insincere.

Pace. Pace yourself. Don't take on more sibling activity than you know you can continue to maintain.

Partnerships. Jointly owned property and partnerships can cause stress between siblings.

Patience. Give your sibling time and space to decide to come back to closeness. It may have taken years for you to grow apart; a few months of patience is not too much to ask for reconciliation.

Patronize. You put down your siblings when you patronize them.

Personality. Allow for personality differences between you and your sibling.

Privacy. When your sibling confides in you keep this information confidential and private.

Problems. Face problems when they surface and sometimes you can stop them before they get larger.

Procrastinate. A sibling who puts off reaching out to an estranged sibling may never recover closeness.

Promises. Never make promises you know you can't keep.

Pry. Don't try to pry into things your sibling wants to keep private.

Question. Whenever possible try to answer your sibling's questions simply and honestly.

Quiet. Let there be quiet times between you and your sibling.

Realistic. Be realistic about progress. Trying sometimes means failing and having to try again.

Reliable. Trust is built on promises kept.

Remind. Keep a calendar marked with important sibling dates to remind yourself not to let other business interfere.

Rules. Don't make exceptions to rules that the two of you have agreed upon.

Schedules. Schedule phone calls, letters, and visits to your sibling on a regular basis and save time for each contact.

Separate. Don't let time and distance separate you from your sibling.

Sorry. When you make a mistake and hurt your sibling don't forget to say you are sorry.

Space. Grown siblings who have separate lives need privacy and space. Too much togetherness can kill off good relations.

Spouse. Guard against letting a spouse drive a wedge between you and your sibling.

Stress. Sibling relationships are vulnerable to stress from outside sources.

Strong. Build on the strong, positive things in your past relationship with your sibling.

Study. Problems should be studied and then solved using what you have learned.

Success. Relationship success calls for renewal of efforts, built up deed upon deed.

Suggest. Never boss your grown sibling. A suggestion should be your strongest promotion.

Telephone. A telephone can be your link back to closeness with a long neglected sibling. Be sure to remember to do more listening than talking.

Thanking. Never let your sibling do something for you and then forget to say thank you.

Thoughtful. Don't extend favors and gifts by rote. Give thought to each contact with your sibling.

Time. Value your sibling's time as you do your own. Never assume you are the only person who is rushed and busy.

Understand. Before making any decisions or statements, try to understand all sides of a situation.

Unity. Build pride in family and a feeling of unity by telling your siblings you are proud of them.

Unlearn. Bad habits that annoy your sibling can be unlearned.

Unwilling. Be unwilling to give up even if your first attempts to begin anew with your sibling are rejected or ignored.

Users. Siblings who are users do not know how to truly love their brothers and sisters.

Vacations. Take short vacations with your sibling to see how things work out before you plan long trips or many days together.

Visit. Ask your sibling if you may visit. When you go to stay with your sibling, be a good guest; bring a gift and don't overstay your welcome.

Voluntary. Volunteer to help your siblings before it is necessary for them to ask for help.

Wait. When you extend a gesture of love, be patient and wait for your sibling's reaction and reply.

X. Siblings can be like the letter X—an unknown quantity. Be flexible about your plans and meet your adult siblings on their own terms.

Yardstick. The feeling you carry in your heart should be all the yardstick you need to measure your relationship with your sibling.

Year-round. Your renewed relationship with your sibling should be a plan with ongoing goals accompanied by year-round diligence.

Yesterday. Love your sibling more today than you did yesterday.

Yourself. Give your sibling part of yourself, your time, your talents, and your love.

Zeal. All contacts with your sibling should be made with interest and zeal. Don't start a plan with less than fully deserved enthusiasm.